**The God many Christians claim to know is not the God of the Bible. It's time we got reacquainted with**

# OUR AWESOME GOD

***A Refresher Course***

REINDER BRUINSMA

**Pacific Press® Publishing Association**
**Nampa, Idaho**
Oshawa, Ontario, Canada

For Danielle and Peter

All scripture references are from the New International Version unless otherwise indicated.

Edited by B. Russell Holt
Designed by Michelle C. Petz
Cover image ©1999 PhotoDisc Inc.



Bruinsma, Reinder.
Our awesome God / Reinder Bruinsma.
p. cm.
Includes bibliographical references.
ISBN 0-8163-1781-X
1. God. 2. Seventh-day Adventists—Doctrines. I. Title

BT102 .B758 2000
286.7'32—dc21

99-087385

00 01 02 03 04 • 5 4 3 2 1

## Contents

# Preface

Sometimes I get a bit discouraged. Church administration undoubtedly has many "ups," but it certainly also has its "downs." I cannot complain about a lack of variation or excitement in my work as secretary of the Trans-European Division of the Seventh-day Adventist Church. Our division covers no less than thirty-eight countries with a challenging array of cultures. Working with fellow leaders—dreaming about the future of the church and making concrete plans to accomplish those dreams—is an inspiring part of the job. But in reality, a great deal of time also has to be spent just moving processes along and extinguishing fires. Consistently, it seems that there is a greater demand for the services of myself and my colleagues when various areas are having problems than when things are moving along nicely.

So I enjoy writing as a welcome change of pace. I especially like to get behind my keyboard and let the creative juices flow when I sense more challenges than opportunities occurring in my administrative duties. Over the years, writing articles and books has given me tremendous joy. Although I have to discipline myself to set aside blocks of time (usually in the early morning hours), it continues to give me great satisfaction to write—either in my native Dutch tongue or, increasingly, in English. It is true that reactions from readers are usually mixed. Any published author will testify that many readers have strong opinions and that they often voice their disagreement in no uncertain terms. I've had my share of negative mail. Once in awhile I've read reviews of my books which, I felt, showed clearly that the reviewer had not read the book very carefully or had misunderstood what I was trying to say.

But any criticism or misunderstanding is far outweighed by the intense pleasure of having someone write or phone to tell me that what I have written has made a positive difference in his or her life. An article I recently wrote for the *Adventist Review* provoked a number of critical letters to the editor. But one brief reaction simply stated, "Your article has made me decide to stay with the church!" Reading that made my day. Not long ago a lady approached me and said, "I just want you to know that after reading your book, I made the decision to return to the church." Such instances are extremely gratifying.

I have been particularly grateful for the many comments I have received from readers of *It's Time. . . to Stop Rehearsing What We Believe and Start Looking for What Difference It Makes*, published by Pacific Press less than two years ago. Many readers have told me, "I can relate to the way in which you approach the doctrines of the church. You have helped me see the relevance of the things we Adventists believe."

I would like to thank the Pacific Press for, once again, taking a chance on me by accepting this new manuscript for publication. It deals with our quest for God—the most fundamental of all questions we human beings can (and should) ask. It has been an intensely rewarding experience for me to struggle with the basics of my own belief in God and to try to put into human words what is far beyond my finite understanding and which will always remain so. I am sure some will find this book too theological or too philosophical. Some, on the other hand, may wish for something more theologically sophisticated. I simply hope that I have succeeded in writing something that is not too difficult for the average reader without formal theological training, but that has enough depth for those who are not content with easy answers.

I hope and pray that the pages of this book will help at least some to catch a clearer vision of our awesome God—the Almighty, triune embodiment of eternal compassion and omnipresent care. He is the God I love and live to serve. I pray that my thoughts will help at least a few others to join me in that commitment to live for God and to love Him unreservedly. He is truly an awesome God.

Reinder Bruinsma
St. Albans, England
February 2000

## Chapter One

# Do Adventists Need a Book About God?

This book is about God. Each year hundreds of books about God are published, so the topic is hardly unique. Does the world really need another book about God?

Even more, this book primarily targets Seventh-day Adventists, and that may raise a few more eyebrows. Why would I target my fellow church members? If I want to write about God, would it not make more sense to write for those who do not believe in Him or who have a wrong concept of Him or only a vague idea of who He is? Furthermore, if I have made up my mind to write for Adventists, would it not, at least, be more advisable to tackle a less "elementary" topic than God? Shouldn't I focus on some more "advanced" aspect of truth?

I don't think so.

It is just as important for Adventists to believe in God—or more specifically, to have a correct concept of God—as it is for anyone else. Neither do I believe that we can simply take it for granted that all Adventists really do believe in the one and only true God. Many, unfortunately, have a concept of God that does not square with what the Bible reveals about Him. All of us—and I most definitely include myself—must constantly ask ourselves whether we are growing in our knowledge of God; whether we are getting closer to Him or are in danger of gradually losing sight of Him.

This need to know more about God has been impressed on me by a statement my son once made. I'll never forget it. At the time, our family was serving a mission assignment in West Africa. This meant that our children had to leave us for their education. Our daughter returned to the Netherlands, our home country, while our son enrolled in an Adventist college in the United States. After his second year, he decided to change his major. This required him to transfer to another Adventist college. As a result, he found himself having difficulty fitting all the required courses into his schedule during his senior year.

Of course, as a student in an Adventist college, he had to enroll in a number of religion classes. His schedule left him few choices, so he ended up taking a class on the harmony of the gospels, a class on the book of Revelation, and an exegesis class on the book of Job. He was clearly interested in religious topics, but repeatedly he expressed to me his disappointment about the classes he had to take. He had been looking forward to taking a course in the basics of Christian ethics, and he would have been quite happy to be exposed to an introduction to the fundamentals of the Christian faith. But his schedule did not allow this. One day he said to me, "I'm not interested in all these complicated things in the book of Revelation. I would like to know more about the existence of God!"

In all honesty, I am still both angry and disappointed that a student at an Adventist college—one who is interested in religion, but who has many fundamental questions—can find himself forced to deal with all kinds of advanced religious topics, but cannot find the opportunity to confront the very basic questions of the Christian faith in any structured way.

My point is that young people, even those who have been raised in an Adventist family and who are attending Adventist schools, may not have settled the number-one question men and women continue to ask: "Does God exist?" I don't believe my son is unique in this regard. I have an inkling—confirmed by discussions with many people, old and young—that he is just one among many.

**Doubt**

In general, many young people are uncertain or doubtful that God exists. Some time ago I found an interesting study of the religious convictions of teenagers in Belgium. Traditionally, Belgium has been a very religious country; practically the entire population used to be Christian—predominantly Roman Catholic, with a small Protestant minority. Many, of course, were Christians only nominally, and more recently a growing number of people no longer consider themselves to be Christians at all. Still, the findings of these studies are shocking. For example, of 336 students, aged fifteen to eighteen, who were asked if they believed in God, only 3.9 percent were absolutely convinced that He exists. Another 28.9 percent believed in God's existence to some extent, but had serious doubts; 44 percent doubted that God exists; 14 percent found it very difficult to believe in God; and 5.4 percent totally rejected the idea that God exists.[1]

Many of these young people, even of those who say they believe in God, will not join the church of their parents. But a considerable percentage will eventually become members. There is an unfortunate trend in Christianity in many places today—growing numbers of believers who no longer belong to a church. At the same time, we are also seeing many who do belong to a church, but who no longer believe. Is Adventism immune from these trends? Why would it be? I know many young people who have been raised as Adventists and who believe in God, but who have never joined the church of their parents or any other church for that matter. I also know many other Adventist young people, however, who have joined the church and who may be quite active in its programs, but whose allegiance to the church is built primarily on social grounds rather than on a strong belief in the God who is worthy of their service.

**Belonging without believing**

It is not only young people who find it difficult to believe in God or who have an inadequate concept of who and what He is. In the Christian world, North America is unique in the fact that an overwhelming majority of its people claim to believe in God. One Gallup poll puts the number as high as 94 percent. The same poll indicates that no less than 84 percent claim to see God as a personal Being, a heavenly Father, who can be reached by prayer.[2] But other research seems to indicate that the number of non-believers in the United States is growing. In America, it has become much more socially acceptable to have no religious affiliation than it has been in the past.

At the same time, those who do believe in God are increasingly confused about Him. According to a recent report, only two-thirds of all Americans now define God as "the all-powerful, all-knowing Creator of the universe who rules the world today." Ten percent refer to God as "a state of higher consciousness," and 8 percent say He is "the realization of all human potential." In addition, millions define God in such terms as, "Everyone is God" or "There is no such thing as God." Others simply don't know what to say when asked about their views of God.[3]

Still, North American figures compare favorably with those of Western Europe. Although Britain claims to be a Christian nation, only about 14 percent of its people are still church members in any active sense. Thirty-two percent of the population claims to believe in a personal God. For the whole of Europe, the figure stands at 39 percent.[4]

But although North American statistics regarding Christian beliefs may appear to be quite favorable, honesty demands that we dig a little deeper. Are all of those two-thirds of the U. S. population who claim to believe in a personal God, truly committed believers? Have they understood what "knowing God" implies? The signals are rather mixed, to say the least. Some 74 percent of all Americans say they want a close relationship with God, yet another set of statistics tells us that about the same percentage of the adult population agrees with the statement: "A comfortable life, enjoyment, and personal fulfillment are the most important things in life." On the average, an American family owns three Bibles, yet only 37 percent of all adult Americans read their Bible at least once a week. And although religion seems, on the surface, such an important ingredient of American life, 38 percent of all adults, at least once a week, see sexually explicit material on video, film, or TV. Even among born-again Christians, 28 percent admit to viewing a weekly dose of X- or R-rated material.[5]

What do these statistics say about the quality of the religious commitment of many who claim to be Christians? Could it be that for many millions their belief in God has remained rudimentary and has not led to a real encounter with the one and only God? Well over half of all born-again young people in America admit that they never talk about their religion with their friends, and about one-third say they have never experienced God's presence in any significant way.[6]

Is the picture any different in the Seventh-day Adventist Church? Possibly a little better. But several studies have shown that in most respects Adventists are not so different from society in general. We live in the same secular environment and are bombarded with the same secular impulses as our non-Adventist neighbors. As Adventists, we do, however, face a few additional temptations.

Our conviction that we have a special message to share with the world has often led us to spend almost all our attention on the "special truths"—Sabbath, Second Coming, the sanctuary, the "health message," the prophecies of Daniel and the Revelation. We have tended to assume that people are aware of the basic Christian teachings—belief in God, in His Son, Jesus Christ, in the Holy Spirit, and in salvation through faith in Christ. Most of our evangelistic outreach in the western world has targeted, and still targets, other Christians. We often take it for granted that the people who hear about the prophecies and the Sabbath and the soon return of the Lord, already believe in the God of the Bible. We simply don't dwell at any length on who and what God is. We just build our special doctrines on the foundation we assume is already there. Could it be, however, that we are assuming too much? Could it be that this foundation, if it exists at all, often may not be very strong and that, as a result, we "win" people who become Adventists without ever becoming solid Christians?

# OUR AWESOME GOD

Should we not make it a higher priority to present God as He is revealed in the Bible, along with the other basic fundamentals of the Christian faith, *before* we present the important implications of those basic beliefs as spelled out in our specific Adventist doctrines?

Unfortunately, there are many Seventh-day Adventists who may know everything about the millennium and who may be able to strongly defend the seventh-day Sabbath and the Adventist position on the state of the dead, but who have the strangest views about God. Often their religion is an allegiance to a system of doctrine rather than a relationship with a personal, almighty, loving God.

**Worshiping a system?**

Early in my career, I pastored a small church in the northern part of the Netherlands where my wife and I came to know one of the prominent members rather better than we had bargained for! This man was determined to visit our home at least once a week. Invariably, he would point out some mistake he had found in an Adventist book or journal. If a journal stated that some event had taken place more than four centuries ago, he would discover that in actual fact only 398 years had passed and that therefore the statement was totally erroneous. If a mission story informed us that a particular town had 1.4 million inhabitants, this member would triumphantly declare that, once again, our church leaders didn't know what they were talking about, since he had established that, in reality, no less than 1.5 million people lived in that town! From time to time I tried to discover what made this man tick. Why did he have this strange obsession with numbers? More than once he explained it to me. "I am an accountant," he would say, "and figures and numbers are what I understand. That is what attracted me to Adventism, all these time prophecies. I can relate to these things. Grace and salvation are too abstract. Numbers are concrete; I can check them to see whether they are correct."

I have never since met an Adventist quite like him, but I have met many who are similar. They became convinced of the truth of Adventism as they heard the rationale for our "special truths." Lectures on archeology helped them to see that the Bible is trustworthy. Presentations on the Bible prophecies helped them to see the deeper meaning of history and played a major role in their decision to dissociate themselves from those who are *wrong* in their teachings, and to join those who are *right* in what they preach. Sermons on the continued validity of the Ten Commandments and other biblical laws caused them to adopt a new life style. It is generally assumed that they are Christians; they have always regarded themselves as such. But how much do they know about God? How well do they know Him? Tragically, often they do not see the need for studying or thinking in-depth about the most important question of the Christian religion (and of Adventism): "How can we be sure that God exists? And if He exists, how can we really know Him?"

I have often heard Adventists complain about the topic of the Sabbath sermon, that it was "just" about God or "just" about the gospel. "These things," they say, "one can hear anywhere. Adventist pastors must not 'waste' their time in the pulpit on these general things, but must preach the three angels' messages!"

When the very basis of the Christian faith is neglected or taken for granted, our worship may easily be the worship of a doctrinal system—worship of a set of truths—rather than a celebration of God's "worth-ship," a deep-rooted response to the "worth" of God. I remember a pastor in one of our churches in the Netherlands who specialized in converting Jehovah's Witnesses. His knowledge of the Watch Tower Society's teachings was impressive. For a while his ministry to members of this community was indeed quite successful; a dozen or so Jehovah's Witnesses decided to join the Adventist Church when they saw that Adventist views were more biblical than their own. But it soon became clear that something was missing; they simply had exchanged one system of doctrinal views for another without ever coming close to the Source of Truth.

This intellectual assent to a set of doctrines without a basic relationship with God usually takes less blatant forms, but it is quite common nonetheless. In fact, historically, the Adventist Church has been much less tolerant of erroneous views regarding the Sabbath, the sanctuary or the prophetic end-time scenario, than it has of heresies concerning the person and the nature of God. An Adventist pastor who openly states that he is not sure that anything special happened in 1844 does not have much future in the denomination's ministry. But his colleague who has problems believing in the Trinity or in the doctrine that Jesus Christ has always existed from eternity, will usually not find his job in jeopardy.

Seventh-day Adventists face another danger. Being an Adventist is an integral part of our identity. Many of us divide humanity simply into "Adventists" and "non-Adventists," as if this is the only distinction between human beings that really matters. Adventists are not hesitant to be critical of their leaders or to speak disparagingly about the bureaucracy of their church, but beneath these criticisms is a solid layer of pride. Their church is special. It has grown against all odds. It now numbers more than ten million baptized Adventists around the world! The church has a network of schools, health institutions, and publishing houses. It is a multibillion dollar enterprise. It has established a presence in almost all countries of the world.

Those who have been church members for many years have invested enormous amounts of time, money, and emotion in their church. Pastors and church administrators have worked for their church, often putting in more hours in a day and more days in a year than is good for their health and their families. They want to see their church successful, and they feel disheartened or even frustrated when the church does not prosper in their part of the world or in their town or village. It is easy, as I know from experience, to be so focused on the well-being of the organization that God, at best, takes second place.

### The "sacred canopy"

Thus, I feel there is ample justification for writing and publishing yet another book about God for an Adventist audience. There are some urgent internal reasons: We need to be constantly reminded of the basis of our religion before we can hope to say, believe, or do anything meaningful about the implications of that faith. But before we go any further, it is also important to place what we have said so far in a somewhat broader context: God is gradually being pushed out of our western world, and that process affects all of us—Christians in general as well as Adventists, and young as well as old.

In the Middle Ages, religion touched all aspects of human life. God was not only linked to what happened in the church, but to every aspect of human existence. People gave religious explanations for the weather, natural disasters, health and illness, the existence of social classes, and even war and peace. The Renaissance, followed by the Enlightenment, brought a gradual, but radical, change. The natural sciences tended to propose non-religious explanations for a wide range of phenomena. With Darwin, the theory of evolution began to replace the Creation account of Genesis 1, 2 as the generally accepted explanation for the origin and development of life on this earth. The "sacred canopy," as sociologist Peter Berger[7] called this link between God and the world of our experience, which had remained unquestioned for as long as mankind could remember, was gradually being removed.

This development demanded a thorough rethinking of God's role. The Christian church and its leaders often displayed a significant degree of panic. After all, if God was no longer necessary as the explanation for a wide range of phenomena, might we not soon see the day when He would be totally superfluous? Theologians did not always react in a balanced way. Some joined forces with the natural scientists, embracing their theories lock-stock-and-barrel, while forgetting that these scientific views were theories and not the last and final word on the subject. Others declared war against the various disciplines of the natural sciences. They defended their traditional views which they regarded as virtually inspired, and remained entrenched in them, unwilling to consider any other perspective than their own.

This discussion about the role of God in the universe and in our world is far from over; it is still at the heart of any debate about the relationship between science and religion. This debate affects every Christian, every Adventist, at all levels of his education, spiritual growth, and his thinking about God.

In addition, there are two other, related facets of modern life. First, our life is thoroughly compartmentalized. In our western society, most of us live a number of parallel lives. Our professional life hardly intersects with our private life. And we may have a third life in sports or in a part-time political career or, indeed, in the church. Our professional life centers around a set of people we will normally not meet in our private life; it may also revolve around a set of values that is quite different from the one we adhere to privately. Many companies will not allow their employees to speak about their religious convictions in the workplace. Having prayer with a colleague would be unprofessional. God belongs to the sphere of private life and must remain absent from the other spheres of our existence.

Second, when people do talk about God, they often express an opinion rather than a passionate belief. Ours is an age of relativism. If something works for you, so much the better! But please allow me to follow my own preferences. There surely must be something good in everything! Let's not pretend that there is just one truth. Let us rather celebrate the rich diversity of beliefs and practices!

As Adventists, we are not immune from the influences of these trends. As Adventists, we live in a world just as secular as that of others around us; our life can easily be just as compartmentalized as that of our colleagues and friends. We also are expected to make our God a private god with a rather restricted sphere of influence. Inevitably, all this may drastically affect our concept of God.

Indeed, there are profound questions about God that puzzle many Adventists, just as they confound others. So much happens in God's name. Wars have been fought, crimes have been committed, people have been brutally killed, children have been taken from their parents, relationships have been tragically destroyed—all in the name of God. What concept of God can possibly justify the injustices committed in His name? How can a God of love ever be called upon to endorse hate and destruction?

We will return to these questions. And we will see that some of the concepts of God held by lifelong, pious Christians are hopelessly inadequate. Their God often more resembles a Santa who is sad when children do not put away their toys in an orderly fashion than the God of the Bible. They seem to be able to believe in a God who, on a weekly basis, dishes out a portion of deadly tumors among His best friends and then has the audacity to expect a compliment. Everything they do not understand they conveniently label as "God's will."[8]

The Dutch Queen Wilhelmina, whose reign included the period when the Nazis occupied her country, made no secret of her belief in God. She is said to have openly praised God for the fact that her son-in-law, Prince Bernhard, had been too sick to travel in a particular aircraft that crashed on the flight he had been scheduled to take.[9] She believed that his life had been saved because God needed him in the war against the Nazis. Many similar stories abound in Christian books chronicling the marvelous ways in which God looks after his people. But if God could save the life of the Dutch prince by preventing him from boarding that plane, could He not with equal ease have prevented the plane from crashing? Or could He not have prevented the rise of the Nazis in the first place?

Generations of Adventist children have read Uncle Arthur's *Bedtime Stories*. They were not available in the Dutch language when I was a kid, but I did not entirely escape their influence. I read quite a few of these stories when I worked as a student literature evangelist and sold Christian books to earn money for my education. The *Bedtime Stories* were among my best sellers. I remember a story about a little girl who had received a watch. But then tragedy struck; the watch was totally demolished when she dropped it and a car ran over it. However, that was not the end of the story. The little girl prayed, and God heard her. Miraculously, the watch was put together again! Well, I believe in God, but, if my watch had been pulverized by a truck, I would count my losses and buy a new one. It would not occur to me to pray to God to miraculously repair my watch. My concept of God does not suggest that He is in the watch repair business. Yet, how many have carried this tragically inadequate picture of God with them into adulthood?

These are legitimate concerns in the minds of many today—of Christians and non-Christians alike. And such questions lead us into the heart of the topic of this book. What is the Christian God like? What can we know about Him? What does He do, and what does He want?

**The ultimate question**

Before we look at these questions, however important they may be, we must first face the ultimate question: Does God exist? Even some Adventists, young and old, are struggling with this fundamental question. I hope that what follows in this book will be of some use to them. But what of those who do not struggle with this doubt somewhere deep down in their hearts? They, too, would do well to review the thoughts about God that we will be considering in these pages. It may help them to share their belief in God with others in a more structured way.

"Does God exist?" is the ultimate question. It is the question about meaning: Where did we come from? Why are we here? Where are we going? We cannot answer these questions without reference to God.

If our existence is the result of mere chance; if there is nothing beyond the material comprising our physical body; if we exist just for a limited number of years and then die; if human life springs from nothingness and ends in nothingness—what is the sense of it all? How can we make moral decisions if there is nothing (or no one) to tell us what is right or wrong? What meaning would there be in creativity and talent, in beauty and order? Without God, what organizing principle would there be for our life?

Of course, humanists claim that they have an alternative for God, but how satisfying is that? The Marxists have proposed their grand dream of a religionless society. However, looking at the countries where the Marxist ideology was adopted, I find little that commends it. For decades Marxism has had its chance, but has it delivered on its promise to provide meaning to its followers?

In this book, I will argue that finding ultimate meaning depends on belief in God—not just belief in any god, but belief in the one and only true God of the Bible.

# Do Adventists Need a Book About God?

In this first chapter, I have occasionally used the terms "argue" or "argument," which may suggest that I am going to involve the reader in a rational debate and that I hope to convince him by the strength of my arguments. That is, however, only partly true. Arguments do have an important place. But they go only so far. Arguments may be able to show that it is not unreasonable to believe in God, and that, in fact, it may be more reasonable to believe in Him than to be an atheist. Likewise, the Bible may help us to clarify our concept of God and to ensure that what we worship is not a god, but the God.

And yet, we can never know that God exists in the same way as we know that the chair on which we sit exists. Our knowledge of God can be only a knowledge of faith. We can only *believe* that God exists. We can only *believe* that He is the almighty, eternal, all-knowing God, the Infinite One. We can only *believe* that His essence is love.

It is possible for someone to list all the rational arguments that speak for God's existence without having a deep-rooted belief that He does indeed exist. Thus, as I write this book, I constantly ask myself the question: Do I personally know God through faith? Do I truly, unconditionally, believe in Him?

Belief in God carries important implications. If He exists, He is my Creator. If He exists, I am totally dependent on Him. If He exists as a personal God, He awaits my response. If I believe that God is love, He not only matters to me, but I matter to Him.

---

1 Dirk Hutsebaut, *Een zekere onzekerheid* (Louvain: Acoo, 1995), 23.

2 Robert Beliza, *Religion in America* (Princeton: The Princeton Religion Research Center, 1993), 20.

3 George Barna, *Virtual America* (Ventura, Calif.: Regal Books, 1994), 109, 110.

4 Grace Davie, *Religion in Britain since 1945* (Oxford: Blackwell Publishers, Ltd., 1994), 47, 78.

5 Barna, 88-90, 49, 36.

6 Quoted in Gary Zustiak, *The NeXt Generation* (Joplin, Miss.: College Press Publishing Company, 1996), 79.

7 Peter L. Berger, *The Sacred Canopy: Elements of a Sociological Theory of Religion* (Garden City, N.Y.: Doubleday, 1967).

8 Okke Jager, *Oude Beelden Spreken een Nieuwe Taal* (Baarn: Ten Have, 1990), 27, 35, 36.

9 *Ibid.*, 37.

Chapter Two

# Incurably Religious

Religious beliefs and practices are found in all contemporary societies. Historians tell us that the same is true for all societies they have studied, and archeologists have found many incontestable signs of religious beliefs among peoples who have left no written records. People in ancient cultures more often than not placed food, tools, and other objects in the tombs of the departed—a clear indication that they believed in some kind of afterlife. Whenever ruins of ancient cities are unearthed, we find not only palaces or other royal dwellings, but also temples and other sanctuaries.

Religion has taken many different forms. People have believed, and still believe, in natural forces and objects that supposedly have special power or significance. They believe in many gods or in one god. The sun, moon, stars, rivers, mountains, rain, and fire have often been identified with deities. There are also many instances of trees or animals of various kinds being worshiped.

Records from ancient Sumer, one of the oldest civilizations known to us, reveal that the Sumerians believed that the universe was ruled by a pantheon made up of a group of living beings, human in form, but immortal and possessing superhuman powers. These beings, they believed, were invisible to mortal eyes and guided and controlled the cosmos in accordance with well-laid plans and duly prescribed laws. The Sumerians had four leading deities, known as "creating" gods: An, the god of heaven, Ki, the goddess of earth, Enlil, the god of air, and Enki, the god of water. They regarded heaven, earth, air, and water as the four major components of the universe. Next in importance to the creating deities were the three "sky" gods, Nanna, the god of the moon, Utu, the sun god, and Inanna, the queen of heaven. Inanna was also the goddess of love, procreation, and war. Other Sumerian gods included those in charge of rivers, mountains, and plains; gods of the cities, fields, and farms; and gods of tools such as pickaxes, brick molds, and plows. Each of the important deities was the patron of one or more Sumerian cities. The citizens erected large temples in the name of their god and worshiped him as the divine ruler and protector of the city.

Ancient Greece offers another fascinating example of a religious system with numerous gods. The Greeks believed that Mount Olympus was home to their gods—Zeus, Hera, Hephaestus, Athena, Apollo, Artemis, Ares, Aphrodite, Hestia, Hermes, Demeter, Poseidon, and a host of others.

Zeus was the most important god, the spiritual father of both gods and humans. His wife, Hera, was the queen of heaven and the guardian of marriage. Poseidon, the brother of Zeus, was ruler of the seas and the god of earthquakes. Greek mythology tells us how these and other gods often behaved in all too human ways. Although the Greeks knew of no official religious organization, they usually honored certain holy places—Delphi being one of the most famous examples. After death, they believed, the soul would go to the underworld, but heroes and great souls would go to the Elysian Fields, while the wicked awaited punishment in the infernal regions. The religion of ancient Rome in many ways reflected the beliefs of the Greeks.

In ancient Mexico, the Aztecs also developed an elaborate religious system with legions of gods and a large priestly class. By performing annual rites, the priests obtained the blessing of the Aztec gods thus preventing the world from collapsing into chaos and darkness. Pyramidal platforms topped by temples dominated the Aztec ceremonial centers. These structures were the stages where the sacrifices—including human sacrifices—were carried out. Some of the features of this religion were quite appalling.

**From many to one?**

These examples, and others that could be added, would seem to indicate that mankind was inclined, as a rule, to worship many gods. In other words, that man originally was a polytheist (*poly*=many; *theos*=god). Indeed, many scholars believe that evolution is not limited to cosmology (the origin and development of the cosmos) or biology, but also extends to mankind's social and even religious development. Religion, they say, developed from a "primitive" worship of objects and spirits, evolved from polytheism (the worship of many gods) to henotheism (the worship of one god to the exclusion of other gods) to monotheism (the belief that only one God exists). Many would then go on to say that this evolutionary process will not be complete until man, one day, has finally outgrown his belief in God and becomes fully independent!

There are serious objections against this theory. Evolutionists have yet to prove many of the basic presuppositions of their theory. But even if they were able to demonstrate beyond reasonable doubt that a full-scale, or at least a substantial, degree of biological evolution has taken place—this would not automatically imply that evolution is also the key to past and present developments in human society or to the study of comparative religion. Furthermore, we must take note of the work of a number of scholars who have found solid arguments for the view that any progression of religious development is more likely to have been quite the reverse of what so often has been uncritically assumed. Considerable evidence exists that in several ancient societies a form of monotheism, in fact, preceded a polytheistic religion.

Several scholars have noted that in ancient cultures the number of deities tended to increase rather than decrease as time went by. Apparently, over a period of time, all kinds of attributes and functions that were once combined in a single particular god or in a few gods, tended to be distributed to a multitude of separate, individual deities. The famous British archeologist and Egyptologist Sir Flinders Petrie (1853-1942) stated unequivocally: "Wherever we can trace back polytheism to its earliest stages, we find that it results from combinations of monotheism."[1] Other research has borne out the same result for ancient China. There are many indications in the written records that ancient Chinese religion "deteriorated" rather than going through a process of "upward evolution."[2]

Father Wilhelm Schmidt (1868-1954), a German theologian and anthropologist who extensively studied the origin of religion, found considerable evidence to support the notion that a form of monotheism preceded the worship of a large pantheon of different gods and goddesses. A condensed English translation of his many-volume work in German appeared in 1930.[3] Schmidt concluded that, if primitive cultures are grouped according to their cultural level, and these groups are then placed in an ascending order, it is found that as these peoples progressed from mere hunters, to food gatherers and storers, to food growers and pastoral nomads maintaining flocks, to settlers or members of semi-urban communities—their religion tended to change from the worship of one Supreme Being to forms of ancestor-worship and polytheism.[4]

To those who believe in the Bible this makes perfect sense. The Bible story has mankind begin in Paradise, in a state of perfection where the first human beings enjoyed a more direct contact with God than we can ever hope to have in this life. God "walked in the garden" and communicated with Adam and Eve face to face (Genesis 3:8). But sin entered the world, and the ensuing chapters in the book of Genesis tell us how man's experiential knowledge of God the Creator became increasingly vague, as he focused on himself rather than on God. Yet, it stands to reason that, as human beings spread over the world, a vague memory of the Creator God, was retained, at least for some time.

### Belief in one God

We must admit, however, that we know precious little about these traces of monotheism in ancient civilizations. One interesting exception is the short emergence of a form of monotheism during the final phase of the New Kingdom in Egypt. Pharaoh Amenhotep IV (1350-1334 B.C.) started a religious revolution by demanding that henceforth only one god be recognized—Aton (or Aten, the sun god or solar disc). Driven by his religious conviction, Amenhotep changed his name to Ikhnaton and moved his capital from Thebes to Akhetaton (now usually referred to as Amarna) where he did not face the same relentless opposition from the priestly class that he had encountered in Thebes. But the new trend died with the king, and the original order was restored when the next Pharaoh ascended to the throne. It was not until about sixteen centuries later that Christianity re-introduced monotheism into Egypt.

Referring to this episode in Egyptian history as a victory for monotheism is, in fact, not totally correct. The worship of Aton did not mean that the existence of other gods was denied. They might still exist, but they were no longer to be worshiped. Only the worship of the sun disc was allowed. This is, of course, a far cry from the monotheism that we find in the three great world religions of Judaism, Islam, and Christianity.

The Old Testament presents to us the God of Judaism. Both Islam and Christianity build on this Old Testament picture of God. As a Christian, I believe that the Christian concept of God is more "complete" (for want of a better word, for how can our concept of God ever resemble completeness?) or "more fully developed" than that of either the Jews or the Muslims. We will say more of the relationship between Yaweh, Allah, and God in chapter 10.

Among the books about God that have appeared in recent years attempting to sketch this development of God in the three monotheistic world religions, two must be singled out: Karen Armstrong's *A History of God*,[5] and Jack Miles's *God: A Biography*.[6] Both have become best-sellers and have, no doubt, influenced the thinking of a lot of people. And they deserve to be successful because they provide fascinating reading about how the Christian God is supposed to have "developed." But, let us make no mistake: The one and only true God has not "developed," "grown," "matured," or "become more sophisticated." These books, in actual fact, report only how man's understanding—the thinking about God by Israelite historians and poets and by Christian theologians—has gradually developed as God continued to reveal Himself in His Word, little by little; and as people who lived within particular historical and cultural contexts were responding to that revelation; and as God revealed Himself "in the fullness of time" in His Son, Jesus Christ.[7]

**Why do so many believe?**

The fact that a belief in God or in many gods has always been, and still is, so widespread demands an explanation. Through the centuries, the questions have been asked: Where does this belief come from? When was religion "invented" or "discovered," or has man always been religious? Those who are willing to trust the Bible have their answer. But some might well argue that we should wait awhile in our discussion before we turn to the Bible. Must not our belief in God precede our belief in the Bible? For if God does not exist, then obviously the Bible is not His Word!

We will soon discover, however, that reason alone does not provide us with a satisfactory answer. All scholarly attempts to solve the riddle of the origin of religion have been unsuccessful. The idea that there is a realm of the divine—Someone or Something far beyond the level of our humanity to which we can somehow relate—has been, and is, mysteriously present in human beings from the very beginning. It does not arise as the result of argumentation. It is just there.

This almost universal sense that there is a God (or gods) to whom we can relate, may be best described as a "basic trust." When we stop to think about it, we realize that we also operate with "basic trust" at the more mundane level of life. For example, most of us will occasionally check the level of oil in our car's engine, but we do not bend over each time before getting into the car to see whether the bolts on all four wheels are still securely fastened. We trust that the people who last changed our tires knew what they were doing. Without the same basic trust that the maintenance crews have done their job, we would hesitate to get into an airplane. When we have broken a leg and need an X-ray, we trust the technician and his equipment; we don't take an expert along to check the diploma of the lab technician and the reliability of the X-ray machine.

Small children normally have this basic trust in their mothers. The baby cries until he feels the breast. Later, he will stop crying when he sees his mother. He has this basic trust that somehow all will be well when mother is there!

The clear fact that the vast majority of mankind, both past and present, have been firmly convinced that there is a divine realm, makes it unreasonable to suggest that faith is merely a disturbance in the human development toward adulthood. One might just as well turn the matter around and view *unbelief* in God as a sign that something is wrong. Could it be that modern man has pushed God out of his world? Could it be that God exists, but that many people have somehow lost the ability to maintain a relationship with Him? Babies only a few days old are unable to react to everything they see. They cannot distinguish one color from another, but they are able to react to the tender presence of a mother. Yet, this child, who can receive signals of love communicated by the mother and who can respond to these signals, may sometimes later in life have certain experiences that render him incapable of giving or receiving love as an adult. Psychotherapists and psychiatrists owe much of their income to this tragic phenomenon. Similarly, could it be that man "by nature" possesses a belief in God as the ground of his being, but that the collective experience of modern man has caused many people to lose sight of Him?

Some theologians in the early church suggested that this almost universal belief in God is the result of a divine spark that each human being receives at the moment of his birth or even at his conception. That idea presents all kinds of difficulties. It can easily lead (and has, in fact, often led) to the view that man has an immortal component that can be separated from the body—the soul which leaves the body when the person dies. But the idea of a divine spark may nonetheless point us in the right direction.

If God exists, and if, therefore, we are His creatures, would it not be reasonable to expect that we have been created, not only with the senses of sight, hearing, smell, and touch and with the capacity to remember, but also with an inexplicable, but undeniable, "basic trust" in Him who created us? Could it be that Richard Dawkins, author of several extremely well-written, popular books on biology, is utterly wrong in proclaiming that we have a "selfish gene," and that we humans are the center of the universe? Could it be, that, in actual fact, we are carrying a "religious gene," a mysterious reminder of our original close communion with the divine?

At this point I can't resist going to the Bible to quote the apostle Paul. When preaching in Athens, he faced a modern audience, always ready to respond to the latest trends. Rather than referring to the Old Testament Scriptures or to words of Jesus, Paul reminded the Athenians of a statement of one of their own poets about the relationship between God and man: "We are his offspring" ( Acts 17:28). From the context it is clear that Paul did not intend to say that there is a mysterious biological relationship between God and man or that man can claim a semi-divine status. It seems that Paul used this fragment of Greek poetry to underline his conviction that man intuitively knows that he is linked to Someone beyond himself! It may well have been Paul's way of saying that human beings are, indeed, incurably religious.

### God: a human projection?

At this point we could proceed to the next chapter were it not for the fact that in more recent history this presupposition—that man's belief in God originates in a Reality beyond himself—has been seriously challenged.

Ludwig Feuerbach (1804-1872) has been called "the father of modern atheism." He proposed in his book, *The Essence of Christianity,*[8] (1841) that God is nothing more than a projection of human ideals. Man created a god who possesses all the qualities human beings lack—supreme knowledge, love, wisdom, and justice. God has no reality; He is the product of human fantasy. Religion is a dream of the human spirit. Human beings must, however, ultimately grow up and reject God. Man must no longer be a slave to his imagination, but must realize that the only real God is man himself.

It is true enough that in thinking about God human beings have often made Him all too human and have, indeed, often created a God who conforms to human ideals and aspirations. To some extent, that is almost inevitable. As we will see, we must therefore, make sure that our contemplation of God is guided by biblical revelation, if we are to avoid a concept of God that is a purely human projection. Feuerbach and his disciples would be correct if they argued that, unfortunately, many humans have indeed created a God in their own image. But Feuerbach surely owes us an explanation why and how peoples of all times, and everywhere, have reacted in much the same way, and how it came about that all of them allegedly invented roughly the same kind of Being. And, even more importantly, the simple fact that people have been prone to make their own projections of God does not in any way prove that, therefore, God does not exist.

A few generations after Feuerbach, the Viennese doctor Sigmund Freud (1856-1939), founder of psychoanalysis, came on the scene. Many of Freud's ideas about the treatment of mental disorders, and, in particular, about the importance of the role of the unconscious and of childhood experiences of sexuality, have withstood the test of time. However, he also tried to explain human religiosity and suggested that religion is merely rooted in "infantile helplessness." Like Feuerbach, Freud believed that God is a projection of the human mind. Man needs someone to lean on, and he, therefore, creates a heavenly father figure whom he calls "God." Again, it must be admitted that, unfortunately, there are people whose concept of God is not much more than the kind of product of the human brain to which Freud referred. But Freud's theory offers no convincing explanation for the sum total of religious experience. The hypotheses of Freud and Feuerbach about religion are assumptions, rather than results demanded by scientific data.[9]

Feuerbach was to have a strong influence on Karl Marx and Marx's faithful friend and disciple, Friedrich Engels, who championed the cause of materialism—the belief that there is nothing besides matter. For Marx, religion was just pie in the sky. People were manipulated into believing in a better hereafter so that they could be exploited in this present life. Belief in God served as "opium for the people," and real happiness would not be attained until all religion had been abolished.

Marxism has been tried on a large scale, and the results of this approach speak for themselves. This materialistic pursuit of happiness led to some ten million deaths under Nazism, more than fifty million deaths during the Soviet experiment, and another thirty million deaths during Mao's Cultural Revolution, not to mention the genocidal atrocities in such places as Uganda (Idi Amin), Cambodia (Pol Pot), Romania (Ceausescu), and Albania (Hoxha) where the atheistic leaders invariably behaved as if they were gods.[10]

Today, Karl Marx has lost most of his following, but some apostles of atheism still have considerable influence. Philosopher Bertrand Russell (1872-1970) has been described as the leading evangelist of anti-God rationalism of the twentieth century.[11] He was a prolific writer on a wide array of philosophical topics; his writings are much more readable for the non-expert than are most other works on philosophy. Colin Brown, an important evangelical critic, points out, however, that the average reader will probably be impressed by Russell's "razor-sharp mind" that "has no difficulty in slicing through" many of the traditional arguments of theologians. He may "be impressed by the cocksure confidence of his [Russell's] generalizations and even dazzled by his parodies of certain aspects of religion." But, Brown continues, "when it comes to the point, [Russell] conspicuously avoids coming to grips with biblical religion." He only "rips a few sayings of Christ out of context!"[12]

In his heyday in the late 1940s, Jean Paul Sartre (1905-1980) was applauded as one of the world's leading philosophers. Like Russell, his literary output was impressive. But what did he have to offer? In one of his main works (with the poignant title *Being and Nothingness*), Sartre maintained that human existence is characterized, in essence, by nothingness. There is nothing in man beyond himself. Man can be free only if he accepts total responsibility for his own decisions—unaided by society, traditional morality, or belief in God. The individual must rely on his own creative powers rather than on any social or religious authority. Historian Paul Johnson points to what has gradually become common knowledge: Sartre's words about heroic secular morality were belied "by the extraordinary squalor, selfishness, confusion, cruelty and not least cowardice of his own life. His final years, in fact, were squalid bordering on the horrific."[13]

The immensely popular biologist Richard Dawkins, already referred to above and especially known for his book *The Selfish Gene*, is one of the best-known contemporary militant "evangelists" of rigid atheism. He argues that it is possible to be an intellectually fulfilled atheist. Dawkins, no doubt, is a prominent biologist and a gifted writer. But like so many other scholars, by moving into theorizing about human life, he has ventured beyond his field of expertise. And it seems that when he does so, his readers are carried along by the force of his professional reputation rather than by convincing arguments.[14]

Other famous advocates of atheism from the past and the present could be mentioned. But the more one reads about them and the more one reads their books, the more one is struck by a strange anomaly: Their work is a life-long commitment to the purpose of proving that life has no purpose![15] Why are many atheists so passionate in their denial of the existence of God? Why can they not simply shrug their shoulders at the ideas of people around them? Or, why can they not simply accept that people have different views? Michael Buckley may well have a point when he says that fear "lies at the origin of religious affirmation, because one feels fragility before the terrors of nature or horror before death. But. . . fear lies [also] at the origin of religious denial: atheism is an attempt to remove the threat of eternal judgment."[16]

How convincing are the champions of atheism after all? Few in recent times have been as aggressive in the struggle against belief in God as Madalyn Murray O'Haire. She campaigned untiringly for the abolition of Bible reading in American public schools, against "Judeo-Christian morality" in the media (I personally fail to see much of this morality in the American media), and against the inscription "In God We Trust" on U.S. currency and coins. She enjoyed calling herself "the most hated woman in America." But, while she was heavily involved in legal proceedings to have the Bible banished from the public schools, her own son, William J. Murray, became a believer in God and an ardent opponent of his mother's influence.

Christian believers are understandably upset by many of the things atheists say about their God, and they shudder at what they consider to be terrible irreverence or even blasphemy. But atheists may have done Christians a major service. The German theologian Heinz Zahrnt has pointed out that modern atheism may well have had a refining and purifying effect on Christian theology. It is worth quoting him at some length:

> Think of the things we took for God! Think of the things we claimed to be the work of God! Think of the things that we have said and done in the name of God! How often have we made God in our own image! From now on this kind of idolatry is impossible. The positive achievement of atheism is the vigorous purification which Christianity, together with its theology, has undergone, bringing the rejection of every kind of idolatry. The French Christian Jean Lacroix once expressed this in the words: "I am grateful to my atheist friends, for they have taught me not to cheat."[17]

**A matter of choice**

Those who believe in the Christian God, Allah, or Yahweh—or in a god or gods of some sort—are by far in the majority. They must, however, admit that there is a significant, and growing minority that does not believe in any being(s) in a higher realm. Formally, the Buddhist are among these, although much popular Buddhism seems to belie this view. But such individuals are also present in significant numbers in the western world. They call themselves agnostics when they want to stress that they have no knowledge of God. Others often prefer the "humanist" label. On the surface they seem more tolerant toward those who have decided to differ from them, but in reality they are usually quite arrogant and condescending when referring to Christians or adherents of other faiths.

People are free to choose. At least that is what those will argue who believe in God as their Creator and who read their Bible. Each human being has the freedom either to choose or reject belief in God. There are, indeed, some serious obstacles to faith in God. But there are, on the other hand, numerous arguments that support belief in the existence of God. There is no scientific way to provide final proof for either position. To believe or disbelieve in God remains a personal choice. We do well to give serious consideration to the things that seem to suggest that there must be a God. And we will do so in the next chapter. But when all is said and done, it remains a matter of choice. For you. For me.

---

[1] Sir W. M. Flinders Petrie, *The Religion of Ancient Egypt* (London: Constable & Co, 1908), 3, 4.

[2] John Ross, *The Original Religion of China*, 25.

[3] Wilhelm Schmidt, *The Origin and Growth of Religion: Facts and Theories* (London: Methuen, 1931).

[4] Arthur C. Custance, *Evolution or Creation* (Grand Rapids, Mich.: Zondervan Publishing House, 1976), Chapter 2, passim.

[5] Karen Armstrong, *A History of God* (London: William Heinemann, Ltd, 1993).

[6] Jack Miles, *God: A Biography* (New York: Alfred A. Knopf, 1995).

[7] Paul Johnson, *The Quest for God: A Personal Pilgrimage*. (New York: HarperPerennial ed., 1997), 37.

[8] Translation of the German *Das Wesen des Christentums*. (New York: Harper, 1957 reprint).

[9] Daniel B. Clendenin, *Many Gods, Many Lords* (Grand Rapids, Mich.: Baker Books, 1995), 46.

[10] *Ibid.*, 47f.

[11] Johnson, 21.

[12] Colin Brown, *Philosophy and the Christian Faith* (Downers Grove, Ill.: InterVarsity Press, 1968), 226f.

[13] Johnson, 22.

[14] Vinoth Ramachandra, *Gods that Fail: Modern Idolatry and Christian Mission* (Downers Grove, Ill: InterVarsity Press, 1996), 83.

[15] *Ibid.*, 83

[16] Michael J. Buckley, 'At the Origins of Modern Atheism', Quoted in: D. Bruce Lockerbie, *Dismissing God* (Grand Rapids, Mich.: Baker Books, 1998), 5.

[17] Heinz Zahrnt, *What Kind of God?* (Minneapolis, Minn.: Augsburg Publishing House, 1972), 45.

**Chapter Three**

# Proofs or Pointers?

Most people do believe in the Christian God or a god of one kind or another. But even those who believe in God may struggle at times with doubt. And Adventists are not excluded from these struggles.

- "Does the God I have grown up with really exist?"
- "What if the things I have always believed in are not true?"
- " What if, in the final analysis, there is no God?"

The debate about whether God exists continues, in a public way between atheists and theists, but often also in the deep recesses of the souls of those who regard themselves as believers.

Does God exist? The answer of many is, "No!" As modern-day disciples of Feuerbach, they suggest that God is a product of our own fantasy and nothing more, a creation of our own immature brains. "God cannot exist," they argue. "Especially not in the way He is usually depicted by Christians. If there were a powerful and loving God, the world would be totally different. How could a good God allow the world to be in such a mess?"

Does God exist? "Yes!" is the answer given by countless others—men and women of all age groups and all walks of life. "Just look around you at the beauty of the flowers and the starry skies and you cannot help but believe in God," they say. "There is no doubt whatsoever; we *know* that God exists. We are in contact with Him. We can listen to Him and talk to Him."

The God-believers, on the one hand, and the agnostics and atheists, on the other, defend their positions with the same passion. The stakes are high for those who believe in God or who want to believe in Him. It is not a question of an insignificant detail in the biography of some eighteenth-century historical figure. It is not a matter of mere speculation about the weather or an abstract evaluation of an object of art. No, the problem of the existence of God is the most fundamental question we can ask. It is the all-important question most people will ask at some stage of their life. God is the bottom line in any discussion about the meaning of human existence.

**Is there any proof?**

One thing is clear—the existence of God is not a question that can be answered in a purely scientific way. In the beginning of this century, a school of philosophy (Positivism) flourished that based itself on the idea that, in judging reality, one can trust only one's senses. Only if you can see, smell, hear, or feel something can you be sure that you are not being deceived. Everything you cannot perceive through the senses must be ignored. Critics of this philosophy were keen to point out that this view has one fatal flaw—the truth of the principle (that only that which can be perceived through the senses is true) cannot itself be tested in the required way! Who can guarantee that only visible, audible, and tangible things really exist? One cannot get that guarantee through seeing, hearing or feeling itself. One has to accept this principle on the basis of the judgment of people who may be very clever, but who are not omniscient or infallible.

A purely scientific answer to the question of the existence of God cannot be given. Of course, there are people who say that nature "proves" there must be a God. We will return to that argument later in this chapter. We shall see that nature does not really provide us with "proof" of God's existence, just as evolutionary scientists cannot say that their scientific studies provide conclusive evidence for the non-existence of God.

**Philosophical "proofs"**

In past centuries (as well as today) there have always been people who wanted to prove the existence of God. So they constructed different arguments for His existence. In the Middle Ages, for example, St. Anselm, the archbishop of Canterbury (c. 1033-1109), constructed a very complex theory about "being." He concluded that someone who thinks logically about the philosophical concept of "being" will inevitably recognize the existence of God. In simple language his argument ran as follows: In thinking about God I have the idea of a perfect being. If this perfect being did not exist, it would not be perfect because it would lack precisely the perfection of existence. It, therefore, exists!

This argument (technically referred to as the Ontological Argument) was strongly criticized by the great medieval churchman and thinker St. Thomas Aquinas (c. 1225-1274) and, later also by the famous philosopher Immanuel Kant (1724-1804). Kant argued that just because I have the idea of a hundred thalers (the currency of his day), doesn't mean that these hundred thalers really exist in my purse. Others have used similar illustrations to make the same point.

Those who are philosophically inclined may still be interested in this sort of argument. But for most modern people, medieval philosophy has become a kind of secret language that has lost most its persuasive power.

**The first cause**

Other arguments for God's existence may impress us more. Many have argued for God's existence on the basis of the law of cause and effect. Each effect has a cause, but what is behind this cause? This cause must itself be the result of another cause, and this latter cause must be the result of yet another cause, etc. You can go on and on, and you will have to conclude, it is argued, that at the very beginning of that long series of causes there must be *a First Cause—God*. This line of reasoning has usually been referred to as the Cosmological Argument.

Others have said, "Look at the order that exists in the universe. Everything has its purpose. Why is this so? There must be something or somebody (God) who has planned everything." This idea is referred to as the Teleological Argument (*telos* is the Greek word for "purpose"). Proponents of this idea often use the example of a watch to illustrate their argument. If one looks at an old-fashioned watch with all its complex springs and gears and wheels, one will have to conclude that there must be a watchmaker! The most famous expression of this line of thinking occurs in the book, *View of the Evidence of Christianity*, written by the famous British clergyman William Paley in 1806. It is worth quoting the opening paragraph of his book in its entirety:

> In crossing a heath, suppose I pitched my foot against a stone, and were asked how the stone came to be there, I might possibly answer, that, for anything I knew to the contrary, it had lain there forever. Nor would it perhaps be very easy to show the absurdity of this answer. But suppose I had found a *watch* upon the ground, and it should be inquired how the watch happened to be in that place. I should hardly think of the answer which I had before given, that for anything I knew the watch might have always been there. Yet why should not this answer serve for the watch as well as for the stone?. . . For this reason, and for no other—that, when we come to inspect the watch, we perceive (what we could not discover in the stone) that its several parts are framed and put together for a purpose, that they are so formed and adjusted as to produce motion, and that motion so regulated as to point out the hour of the day. That, if the different parts had been differently shaped from what they are, or placed in any other order than that in which they are placed, either no motion at all would have been carried on in the machine, or none which would have answered the use that is now served by it. . . . The inference is inevitable, that the watch must have had a maker, [and] that there must have existed an artificer who formed it for the purpose which we find it

> to answer; who comprehended its construction, and designed its use.[1]

Or take another example which illustrates the same thought: Suppose a traveler in a dense forest suddenly comes to an open space with a nicely kept house, surrounded by a beautiful garden. The traveler will have to conclude that there must have been someone who built this house and who planted the garden.

These arguments address a basic question that simply will not go away: Is the universe sufficient within itself? Why is there something rather than nothing? Why and how does the universe exist? Why is it apparently organized, at least to a significant degree? Voltaire once said: "The universe embarrasses me, and I cannot think that this clock goes without a clock maker."[2] Kant was not totally convinced by this argument, but remarked nonetheless: "This proof always deserves to be mentioned with respect. It is the oldest, the clearest and the most accordant with the common reason of mankind!"[3]

**Morality**

There are still other "proofs." They are rooted in the inner reality of the human spirit. Human beings, it is said, have by nature an idea of God. They remain inwardly dissatisfied until they become aware of the effective presence of God in them. Confronted with this argument, one cannot help but hear the echo of the immortal words St. Augustine (354-430) penned in his *Confessions*: "You [God] have made us for Yourself, and our heart is restless until it finds rest in You."

A similar argument runs as follows: Man somehow knows the distinction between good and evil. He may sometimes be confused about what is "good" and what is "bad," but he knows that at some point a line must be drawn between those two categories. Somehow, the conscience of the vast majority of people listens to a moral law. If there is such a "law," then there must also be a "law-giver"—God.

Opinions differ regarding the value of these types of arguments. They are not without value, but neither are they totally convincing. They may indeed lead to the logical conclusion that there must be something higher than ourselves, but this does not mean that one can prove the existence of a God who resembles the personal, almighty God of the Christian faith.

It seems that the traditional arguments for the existence of God mostly impress people who already believe in Him. People who are already convinced that God exists will nod in agreement when they hear these traditional arguments. But those who do not believe will not easily be persuaded by them.

Yet, we should not dismiss these arguments too quickly. If some of the greatest thinkers of all times have seen value in them, perhaps we should give them more weight than is currently fashionable among many modern thought leaders.[4] The "proofs" may not be totally conclusive, but they make us think. Lutheran bishop Walter Kasper refers to them as "argued invitations to faith."

True, we cannot verify God concretely or experimentally. Unlike astronomers and astrophysicists, whose radiotelescopes can demonstrate mathematically, experimentally, and concretely that the earth is a minuscule grain of dust lost in a gigantic galaxy, itself lost in the midst of countless millions of other galaxies equally gigantic, believers cannot offer irrefutable, scientific proof of God's existence. But although there is no absolute, scientific proof for the existence of God, there is also certainly no scientific proof for atheism. Science has not proven that there is no God! To affirm God's existence is at least as logical and consistent as it is to deny that He exists.

Richard Swinburne, Oxford professor of philosophy of the Christian religion, makes this point over and over again in his recent book *Is There a God*?[5] In this modest, but profound, treatise he builds a strong case for the reasonableness of belief in God. First, Swinburne analyzes the basic criteria for any valid scientific theory and then points out that belief in God satisfies these very criteria. Science has made great progress in explaining the *how* of things, but must remain silent about the *why* of things. Swinburne maintains that God is by far the simplest and most coherent basis—far simpler and far more coherent than either materialism or humanism—for ultimately explaining the universe and all phenomena in it.

Swinburne believes that Darwin's theories about the origin of life are basically true. But, even if that is admitted (and many Bible-believing Christians, Adventists among them, would not be willing to do so), Darwin can point only to a "Big Bang" as the explanation for the *how* of the origin of the universe; he can point only to some "primitive soup" for the *how* of the first traces of life on this planet. But neither he, nor any scientist before or after him, can explain the *why*.[6] Science sees the order in the universe; it can analyze it, but it cannot explain it. How scientific is it, after all, to say that everything comes from nothing?

The traditional "proofs" show that it makes eminent sense to believe in the existence of God; they provide a reasonable explanation for the fundamental aspects of reality. They show that the idea of God is intelligible and is the most coherent and comprehensive interpretation of life and reality available to us. At the very least, the various arguments for God establish belief in His existence as an intellectually responsible position.[7]

### Faith

But, interesting and meaningful though the "proofs" may be, they are not conclusive. Other explanations, although perhaps even less conclusive, remain possible. Accepting or rejecting God is therefore a matter of faith. If there were total, unequivocal, absolute evidence for God's existence, no faith would be needed. On the other hand, if there were total, unequivocal, absolute evidence that God does not exist, faith would be impossible. It would be impossible to have faith in defiance of all evidence![8]

Faith must remain faith, but according to the famous dictum of St. Anselm, "Faith seeks understanding." The author of the New Testament letter to the Hebrews connects faith and understanding ("proof") in an intriguing way: "By *faith* we *understand* that the universe was formed at God's command" (Hebrews 11:3, emphasis supplied). Faith in God is not irrational, yet it cannot be reduced to what we can grasp with our reason.

The "proofs" are important, but they may be dangerous if they are detached from faith. An attempt to prove God's existence by purely rational arguments may sometimes weaken confidence in God's reality rather than strengthen it. Stressing the validity of the "proofs" has usually led to vehement attempts to disprove them. It has even been suggested that modern atheism resulted, at least in part, from the willingness of theologians to relegate the question of God's existence to the arena of philosophical discourse where it became totally detached from faith.[9]

But something else needs yet to be said. Even if the "proofs" were totally conclusive, they would not necessarily lead to the biblical concept of God. They might perhaps lead to belief in a supernatural, all-powerful Being, to a First Cause, a Prime Mover, a "Ground of our Being" (the term theologian Paul Tillich popularized), but they would not lead us to the personal, loving God of Christianity, who is the Father of our Lord Jesus Christ. Even Calvin, who believed that there is a "seed of religion" in every human being which is at the root of the universal presence of religion in all human cultures, warned that this innate sense of divinity will lead, at most, to a confused knowledge of God that inevitably will be distorted by superstition or rebellion.[10]

The next chapter forms a bridge to a closer look at what we may know by faith about the Christian God as He is described in the Bible and as He is more directly presented to us in Jesus Christ. We shall see that there are many gods masquerading as the true God. Once we have unmasked them as idols, totally unworthy of our praise and prayer, we can move on to an encounter with the one and only true God in chapters five, six, and seven.

---

[1] Cooper, Bill, ed., *Paley's Watchmaker* (Chichester, England: New Wine Press, 1997), 29, 30.
[2] Quoted in Dominique Morin, *How to Understand God?* (London, SMC Ltd, 1990), 75.
[3] Immanuel Kant, *Critique of Pure Reason,* (English translation; London: Macmillan, 1933), 520.
[4] For a popular but insightful discussion, see Dominique Morin, *How to Understand God?* (London, SMC Ltd, 1990), 73-80.
[5] Richard Swinburne, *Is There a God?* (New York: Oxford University Press, 1996).
[6] Swinburne, 58ff.
[7] For a profound discussion of the reasonableness of belief in God by an Adventist theologian, see Richard Rice, *Reason and the Contours of Faith* (Riverside, Calif.: La Sierra University Press, 1991), 123-165.
[8] *Ibid.*, 62-66.
[9] *Ibid.*, 202f.
[10] *Ibid.*, 110.

**Chapter Four**

# Will Any God Do?

The stories are well known, but let me briefly retell them in case some readers are a bit hazy on the details. One story is from the Old Testament, and one is from the New Testament. Both make the same point.

During the period of the judges, we find the tribes of Israel locked into an almost constant struggle with the peoples that were still occupying parts of the land the Israelites believed God had promised to them. Among these peoples, the Philistines are probably the best known to the modern Bible reader. The Philistines lived in the coastal region of biblical Palestine, in what we, today, call the Gaza Strip. Their supreme god, Dagon, was not just one of many small-time gods; he was, in fact, more or less identical with the famous Baal. He was a grain and fertility god whose most famous temples were at Gaza and Ashdod. With the recent discovery of documents at ancient Ebla in Syria, it is clear that Dagon was a very ancient and prominent god. These texts show that Dagon was being worshiped in Canaan before Abraham entered the land about 2000 B.C., and he continued to be worshiped by the Canaanites up to the time of Christ.

First Samuel 5 tells us that toward the end of the era of the judges the

Philistines once again gained the upper hand over Israel. To the Philistines, this clearly meant that their god, Dagon, was obviously more powerful than Israel's God. In order to underline the superiority of their god, they brought the holiest object of the Israelite religion, the ark of the covenant, into the temple of Dagon.

What happened next is most interesting. The God of Israel entered into the spirit of the Philistines' game and gave the arch-enemies of His people a lesson that is as powerful as it is humiliating: He is the true God, and this Dagon-god is nothing. Ellen White graphically describes the scene:

> In the morning, the priests . . . entered the temple, and they were terrified to find Dagon fallen upon his face to the ground before the ark of the Lord. They raised Dagon and placed him in his former position. They thought he might have accidentally fallen. But the next morning they found him fallen as before upon his face to the ground, and the head of Dagon and both his hands were cut off. The angels of God, who ever accompanied the ark, prostrated the senseless idol god, and afterward mutilated it, to show that God, the living God, was above all gods, and that before Him every heathen god was as nothing.[1]

The second story—the New Testament one—takes us to Athens. We find it recorded in Acts 17. Somehow it has a very modern ring to it, seemingly reflecting sections of our society today, when it says that "all the Athenians and the foreigners who lived there spent their time doing nothing but talking about and listening to the latest ideas" (verse 21).

The apostle Paul made a stop in Athens during his third missionary journey. There he preached the gospel of Jesus Christ as forcefully and convincingly as he could. He argued for days with his audience, using all the contextualized arguments he could muster, even to the extent of quoting from their own Greek poets. He understood how his God had to compete with the numerous gods of the pagan Greeks. Just read the following few verses from Acts 17:

# Will Any God Do?

While Paul was waiting . . . in Athens, he was greatly distressed to see that the city was full of idols. So he reasoned in the synagogue with the Jews and the God-fearing Greeks, as well as in the marketplace day by day with those who happened to be there. A group of Epicurean and Stoic philosophers began to dispute with him. Some of them asked, "What is this babbler trying to say?" Others remarked, "He seems to be advocating foreign gods." They said this because Paul was preaching the good news about Jesus and the resurrection. Then they took him and brought him to a meeting of the Areopagus, where they said to him, "May we know what this new teaching is that you are presenting?"

Paul then stood up in the meeting of the Areopagus and said: "Men of Athens! I see that in every way you are very religious. For as I walked around and looked carefully at your objects of worship, I even found an altar with this inscription: TO AN UNKNOWN GOD. Now what you worship as something unknown I am going to proclaim to you. The God who made the world and everything in it is the Lord of heaven and earth and does not live in temples built by hands. And He is not served by human hands, as if He needed anything, because He Himself gives all men life and breath and everything else.

"For in Him we live and move and have our being." As some of your own poets have said, "We are his offspring." Therefore since we are God's offspring, we should not think that the divine being is like gold or silver or stone—an image made by man's design and skill (verses 16-29).

### God versus idols

Will any god do? These two stories of the confrontation between Dagon and the God of Israel and between the Athenian gods and the God preached by Paul suggest otherwise!

Yet, many people today feel that most gods will do. People wonder about, or are outright suspicious of, the claims of those who trumpet their religion as the only true, saving faith and who market their doctrines as the final word about God. More and more, people tend to feel that all religions are basically the same. They may be different in the way they portray God and eternity; they may prescribe a different kind of lifestyle and suggest a different type of religious experience and worship, but deep down they all are historically and culturally conditioned responses in the same human search for the Beyond. And if there is a heaven, a nirvana, or a future paradise of some sort, all religions will eventually lead us there. The medieval world had a saying: "All roads lead to Rome." Likewise, many believe today that all religions lead to God.

This idea that everyone will eventually inherit whatever future life awaits us is not new. There has been a "universalist" stream among Christians throughout the ages, whether or not they have labeled themselves as such. Today a vigorous debate is raging among Christian theologians, particularly among those who specialize in the science of missions, whether the Christian faith is unique or is simply one world religion among others. We will return to this important issue in chapter ten.

The Bible, however, clearly points us in a different direction. The two stories referred to above—and many others could be added—leave no doubt. The God of the Bible is not content with His own reserved slot among the many other gods that have been worshiped in the past and who are still being worshiped today. "For all the gods of the nations are idols, but the Lord made the heavens" (Psalm 96:5).

The God of the Bible is not even satisfied with preferential treatment. He is a "jealous God" (Exodus 20:5) who insists on being worshiped as the only genuine God. Whoever or whatever competes with Him is not divine as He is, but is simply an idol. There is no half-way house. On the one hand there is the true God, and on the other hand there is a vast array of phenomena—natural forces, products of human skill and fancy, ideals, ideas, animals, or human beings—that must be classified as non-gods or even demonic. G. K. Chesterton once remarked that when a man turns his back on God, he does not then believe in nothing, but he tends to believe in anything. The so-called secular world of modern men and women, no less than the traditionally religious world, is heavily awash with gods.[2]

It is important to be clear about the definition of idols. When we hear the word "idol," most of us think of the statues of gods and goddesses we have seen in museums or of the images we have seen on the walls of Egyptian temples, or of the illustrations in books on classical mythology. The Bible repeatedly refers to that kind of idol and time and again makes the point that the value of these artifacts is limited to the materials that have been used to make them. The words of Psalm 115 are full of biting sarcasm:

> Why do the nations say, "Where is their God?" Our God is in heaven; He does whatever pleases Him.
>
> But their idols are silver and gold, made by the hands of men. They have mouths, but cannot speak, eyes, but they cannot see; they have ears, but cannot hear, noses, but they cannot smell; they have hands, but cannot feel, feet, but they cannot walk; nor can they utter a sound with their throats (verses 2-7).

The prophet Isaiah echoes a similar sentiment:

> All who make idols are nothing, and the things they treasure are worthless. Those who would speak up for them are blind; they are ignorant, to their own shame.
>
> Who shapes a god and casts an idol, which can profit him nothing? . . . The blacksmith takes a tool and works with it in the coals; he shapes an idol with hammers, he forges it with the might of his arm. He gets hungry and loses his strength; he drinks no water and grows faint. The carpenter measures with a line and makes an outline with a marker; he roughs it out with chisels and marks it with compasses. He shapes it in the form of man, of man in all his glory, that it may dwell in a shrine. He cut down cedars, or perhaps took a cypress or oak. He let it grow among the trees of the forest, or planted a pine,

> and the rain made it grow. It is man's fuel for burning; some of it he takes and warms himself, he kindles a fire and bakes bread. But he also fashions a god and worships it; he makes an idol and bows down to it. Half of the wood he burns in the fire; over it he prepares his meal, he roasts his meat and eats his fill. He also warms himself and says, "Ah! I am warm; I see the fire." From the rest he makes a god, his idol; he bows down to it and worships. He prays to it and says, "Save me; you are my god" (44:9-17).

Idols are not limited, however, to artifacts of precious materials or stone used as objects of worship. Dictionaries stress that there is an additional meaning: *A person or a thing that is the object of excessive adulation.* We should not make the mistake of thinking that because our western world has relegated the images and statues of ancient gods to museums, it has thereby done away with all idols. The following words, though written over a century ago, provide a clear-cut definition of idolatry and aptly describe the present situation:

> An idol is anything that human beings love and trust in, instead of loving and trusting in the Lord their Maker. Whatever earthly thing men desire and trust in as having power to help them and do them good, leads them away from God, and is to them an idol. Whatever divides the affections, or takes away from the soul the supreme love of God, or interposes to prevent unlimited confidence and entire trust in God, assumes the character and takes the form of an idol in the soul temple.[3]

Though in a different form, idolatry exists in the Christian world today as verily as it existed among ancient Israel in the days of Elijah. The god of many professedly wise men, of philosophers, poets, politicians, journalists—the god of polished fashionable circles, of many colleges and universities, even of some theological institutions—is little better than Baal, the sun-god of Phoenicia.[4]

# Will Any God Do?

## Secular gods

What are some of the modern gods that vie for the allegiance of today's masses? First, we can point to a long list of people who are treated and worshiped as gods. A few examples, chosen at random, suffice to illustrate how widespread this phenomenon is. I have often wondered why millions have traveled to Graceland, near Memphis, to visit the grave of Elvis Aron Presley (1935-1977), the king of rock-and-roll. Checking my *Encarta '98 Encyclopaedia*, I learned that Elvis's "romantic, suggestive ballads were matched by his erotic gyrations on stage, characteristics that made him one of the first mass idols of US adolescent culture." If ever there was a global idol, it was Elvis!

And what about Madonna Louise Veronica Ciccone, better known simply as Madonna? Does she owe her idol-status to her talents as a singer or film star? Or to the constant flaunting of her sexuality and her often outlandish behavior? Whatever the basis of her popularity may be, Madonna is worshiped by millions. And so are the Spice Girls, the British pop phenomenon that took Great Britain, North America, and the Far East by storm in a way not seen since the Beatles (who were, and still are, idols in their own right). It is estimated that the Spice Girls earned more than $50 million in 1998.

Mentioning such stars as Marlene Dietrich, Brigitte Bardot, Gina Lollobrigada, Sophia Loren, and Elizabeth Taylor would be meaningful only for the fifty-plus generation and would betray my own age.

But the popular idols of today's world are certainly not limited to stars of music and film. Just as popular, or even more so, are the idols of politics (Kennedy, Reagan, Mrs. Thatcher) or of sports. The fact that soccer players are "sold" to other clubs for millions of dollars and earn tens of thousands of dollars per week clearly underlines their semi-divine status.

But if we really want to grasp the attraction of modern gods and goddesses, we need to look at some aspects of life that have assumed an inordinate place in society and are indeed (as the dictionary phrased it) receiving "excessive adulation." In far too many hearts they have taken first place and have effectively pushed the one and only God aside. I am referring to money, work, sex, and power.

It is often argued that money is neutral, that it can be used for good things as well as for bad things, but that it is neither good nor bad in itself. In theory this may be true, but in actual practice it seldom proves to be the case. Money can indeed be used in positive ways. In evangelical circles we often hear about the "kingdom use" of money. Money has influence. It has purchasing power. We say: "Money talks." But Bob Dylan corrects this: "Money does not talk," he says. "Money swears." Money is animated, energized by "powers," another author contends.[5] Jacques Ellul (1912-1994), the well-known French Protestant theologian, philosopher, and political and social scientist, stresses the same point, describing money as a material and spiritual power that possesses an active and seductive force.[6]

When Jesus used the Aramaic term "Mammon" to refer to wealth, He gave it a personal and spiritual power and underlined that it is a rival god—a power that seeks to dominate us. In His parable about the unfaithful steward, Jesus left no doubt—we cannot serve both God and money. It is the One or the other (Luke 16:13). That is also why Jesus was so tough with the young ruler who wanted to follow Him. The young man had to get rid of his material possessions since they clearly had become a rival god (Luke 18:18-27). This is also why Jesus cleansed the temple—because the religion of the nation had to be purged of its Mammon worship.

In her day, Ellen G. White noted that Mammon was the idol of many. "The love of money, the desire for wealth," she writes, "is the golden chain that binds them to Satan. . . . But these slavish bands must be broken. We cannot be half the Lord's and half the world's. We are not God's children unless we are such entirely."[7]

I am not sure whether Ellen White was primarily thinking of her fellow church members when she wrote these words or of the populace at large. But the fact is that Adventists today would do well to pay heed to these words. For Christ's statement that we cannot serve God and Mammon applies also to contemporary Adventism, to individual church members, and to the corporate church alike.

Money plays a very important role in the lives of many Adventists, even of many pastors and other church employees. The system of paying every church worker a reasonable wage that provides a modest, but reasonable, standard of living has been under serious attack of late. Various categories of workers have been able to break away from the church's traditional philosophy of remuneration and now earn what "the market" demands. I must be careful not to condemn people too easily, but from my observations it would appear that many are dangerously close to attempting to serve both their God and their pocketbook.

Another serious concern related to money should be mentioned. Although all brothers and sisters in the church are supposed to be equal, it seems to me that the church has developed a distinct adoration for the rich and the very rich in its midst. Those who are willing to make sizable donations and those who are regarded as potential donors are often put on a pedestal because of their wealth. There is no doubt: Even in the Adventist Church, money speaks loudly. And although (to refer to Dylan's words) Adventist money does not swear, it certainly does persuade and exert influence. As Adventists, we must seriously ask ourselves whether money has not in many cases become an idol in our midst.

The same is true for work. The Adventist lifestyle may help prevent lung cancers and alcoholism, but it does not keep us from becoming workaholics. Often we seem to be able to get away with this. Is not hard work, even excessive work, at all hours of the day and the week, a sign of our dedication? Many church employees talk derisively of those who are prepared to work only the hours for which they have contracted. Some brag about the fact that they have no time to take a vacation, that they are simply too busy doing the Lord's work.

In general, Adventists seem to be rather Calvinistic in their work ethic. We are achievers. Work is a not just a means of earning a living—it is a calling. Christian stewardship demands that we deliver our very best and that we scrupulously use our time in a profitable way. Robert Wuthnow warns that workaholism is sinful; it marks a grave misunderstanding of one's relationship with God. When we create an idol out of our work, we tragically forget that we owe allegiance only to the Lord! Wuthnow goes on to say that the Christian worker is particularly susceptible to workaholism. A high degree of conscientiousness, a refined sense of accountability, and a frequent misinterpretation of the Protestant work ethic as requiring excessive working hours—all these are risk factors for the disease and addiction of overwork.[8]

By focusing on Adventists, I am not for a moment suggesting that the idol of work is not a problem for the world at large. It is, unfortunately, an infatuation we share with millions of our fellow citizens.

But what about yet another idol—sex?

Sex is so all pervasive and so aggressively present in our world and seems to dominate the lives of so many millions, that it certainly qualifies as an idol. Today when many people use the word "love," more often than not they mean simply "sex"—lust, without commitment or intimacy. Escort services or less sophisticated forms of prostitution, X-rated films, juicy Internet sites and adult videos and magazines are only the most explicit part of the equation. Advertisements of clothing and toiletries—but also of washing powders, cell phones, and cars—apparently require a solid dose of soft-sex to be effective. And more recently, all kinds of things are labeled as "sexy." The worship of sex not only tends to destroy the capacity for true love, but also comes with huge social costs—abuse of children, violence against women, broken marriages, the destruction of family life, and exploitation of the weak and vulnerable.

Christians—Adventists included—do not live on another planet, and they cannot help but be affected by the exploitation of sex in the western world. As a result, no doubt some have moved from a healthy experience of their sexuality to idol worship.

But the list of idols is longer than money, work and sex. Paul Tillich once remarked that human beings are factories of idols, whether physical objects or mental concepts. Millions worship their body as their supreme idol, and devote a lot of time and energy to the rituals of sports or working out. Others worship the idol of power, sometimes as unobtrusively as possible or even under the guise of servitude (could this apply to a few Adventists?), but sometimes also quite blatantly.

Others look to science as their idol. Many scientists are sincere and humble Christians, but men such as Huxley, Herbert Spencer, and Auguste Compte turned science into a new religion. In some countries, such as China, the worship of science has enthralled a major portion of the population. Vinoth Ramachandra, a theologian who lives and works in Colombo, Sri Lanka, has rightly observed that the scientific enterprise must be ruled by love. When love is absent, science easily becomes demonic, and when divorced from the biblical worldview it leads to irrational idolatry.[9]

And, of course, we cannot forget a whole range of philosophies, economic theories, and political systems that have become doctrines demanding total commitment and that are often worshiped in a quasi-religious way. For many, capitalism, with its adjuncts of a totally free market economy and a laissez-faire attitude, easily falls into that category, as does Marxism, socialism, and communism on the other hand, for many others.

### In the name of God

A prominent feature of idolatry is the use of gods or God for our own purposes. Look at the "primitive" peoples and their gods. These gods were supposed to bring rain or sunshine. They were supposed to help win a war against a neighboring tribe. They were supposed to bestow fertility and give many sons and daughters. Compare this with our modern idols of money, sex, and power, for example. They, too, are supposed to put our lives in top-gear and ensure that we are really "living."

Unfortunately, we have to confess that we have often relegated the Christian God to the realm of an idol. Idolatry is not only the mistake of identifying God with some physical reality and worshiping a human artifact or a mental concept; idolatry also includes trying to limit, manipulate, or control God and thus attempting to make Him serve our own purposes.[10]

It may be somewhat uncomfortable for us to recognize the fact that many Christians often invoke their God as if He were a rain god or a fertility god of old. They approach Him when they need or want something badly. They come to Him when they are in a bind and are looking for a way out. They pray to Him when they feel sick or when a loved one is in trouble. They want Him to win their wars for them and make them victorious. It is indeed a basic tenet of the Christian faith that God answers prayer and that there is nothing, whether it be something earth shaking or seemingly insignificant, that we cannot bring to Him. But prayer without a relationship with God, or at least without the desire to establish such a relationship, is nothing more than idolatry—making God into an object that can be taken from the heavenly shelf when we decide we have use for it.

The fact that people invoke God's name for all sorts of activities does not necessarily mean that the true God is actually involved in any way. Asking for God's blessing on something we have already decided to do is not necessarily an act of worship; often it can be an act of clever manipulation, idolatrous propaganda, or self-deception.

All kinds of horrible things have been done in the name of God. It is not difficult to prepare a catalogue of the dark side of Christianity. Cultures of indigenous peoples around the world have been destroyed in the name of God, supposedly because they were pagan, but mostly because the westerners who wanted their land did not understand their way of life and felt infinitely superior. Guns, cannons, tanks, and battleships have been blessed in the name of the Christian God by His representatives of various persuasions. Again and again throughout history, Jews have been massacred in that same name; after all, so the argument ran, they were the ones who had killed Christ and therefore deserved no mercy. Thousands of women have become the victims of Christian witch hunts—the famous episode in Salem, Massachusetts, in the bleak winter of 1691 being just one example of this terrible crime, albeit the most famous. In the name of God, Christian leaders and believers have felt more than justified to rid themselves of the demonic in their midst!

Protestants long remembered (and still do in some quarters) how inquisitions sponsored by the church-state persecuted "heretics" who happened to believe something that deviated from official church teachings. These inquisitions gave their victims the choice: recant or be executed, and did it all in the name of God. But before we fuel any dormant anti-Catholic sentiments, we would do well to remember that Protestants have demonstrated their own share of intolerance. Michael Servetus, the Spanish doctor and theologian who was burned at the stake in Geneva in 1553 because of his heretical ideas about the Godhead, was perhaps the most famous victim of Calvinistic Protestant persecution. But the early history of Puritanism in the United States also had its examples of a terrible intolerance that has tainted the annals of a nation presumably founded on a deep longing for freedom from political and religious oppression. But whatever happened in these persecutions and whoever was the persecuting power, almost invariably all was done in the name of God.

If Protestants are gradually forgetting what the Inquisition sought to accomplish in the name of God, the Muslims certainly have not forgotten the Crusades, those murderous campaigns to save the "holy" lands of the Bible from occupation by the followers of Mohammed. It may now be more than nine centuries since Pope Urban II preached his stirring sermon in the French city of Clermont (1095), but his words have not been forgotten. "It is the will of God," the pope said. "Let these words be your war cry when you unsheathe your sword. You are the soldiers of the cross. Wear on your breasts or shoulders the blood-red sign of the cross. Wear it as a token that his help will never fail you, as the pledge of a vow never to be recalled."[11] And thus the slogan *Deus vult*—God wills it—became the banner for the most shameful enterprise Christians have ever engaged in.

In the name of God, religious communities have been torn asunder by people whose doctrines often were considerably more pure than were their motives and who below the surface were at times more intent on making a name for themselves than on defending the Name they were invoking. In the name of God, families have been destroyed, lives have been disrupted and ravaged, and people have been emotionally damaged for life. In the name of God, people have been told to conform, to deny innocuous pleasures, to submit to all kinds of extreme dietary regimes.

They have been pressured to obey the dictates of pastors, teachers, parents, and friends, who unconsciously or subconsciously (or even consciously), sincerely or cunningly, have made the God they claim to serve into an idol which expresses their own thoughts rather than anything divine. (Do I really need to elaborate on this further and point out how this type of idolatry can easily find its way into the Adventist Church?)

### A partisan God

A variant of the kind of idolatry we have been examining is the one that makes the Christian God into a totally partisan God—a God who is fully on our side and totally against the side we consider as the enemy. Critics of the Christian religion have often pointed to the anomaly of parties in opposite camps both assuming that God is their Supreme Ally. During World War II, priests were blessing the guns of the Axis powers, while their colleagues in the West assured the members of the Resistance Movement that God would be with them in their divinely appointed mission.

This is nothing new. From the moment Emperor Constantine saw the mysterious shape of a cross in the sky and heard the voice say: "In this sign, conquer!" he knew that God was his Ally. And ever since, kings and emperors, generals and admirals, presidents and prime ministers—and even tyrants and dictators—have vowed to their followers that God was with them. Many a national anthem still breathes this sentiment.

Living in Great Britain, I have followed for years the developments in Northern Ireland with keen interest. I must admit I find it difficult to control my feelings of utter repulsion when I hear the Reverend Ian Paisley shout his vitriolic condemnations of the British government which, in his view, has sold out to "the papists." How he thinks of Catholicism is evident from the title of the book he wrote in 1982: *No Pope Here!* Supported by the approximately 20,000 members of the Free Presbyterian Church of Ulster, which he founded in 1969, and by the members of his political party, he knows exactly what side God is on—his side!

# Will Any God Do?

But this phenomenon is not a British invention. Americans, possibly more than the citizens of any other nation, have had a tendency to think that God is always on their side, and this has not diminished in recent years. Was not America the only credible antidote against the evil empire of Communism? And at present is America not the only remaining world power that can ensure a measure of order and justice in the world and protect freedom of belief around the globe? In particular, many people who lean toward the right of the political spectrum and who align themselves with the Christian Coalition and similar organizations, tend to be firmly convinced that God is totally on the side of America. They would argue that they are intent on serving His purpose, but those looking on from outside are just as sure that, in fact, God's role in this scenario is to serve the party and political schemes of the right.

People with completely opposite programs are adamant that God is in their camp. This reminds us of the predicament of the American people at the time of the Civil War. Which side could reckon on divine support? Julia Ward Howe (1818-1910), the Unitarian campaigner against slavery from Boston, voiced the sentiments of the Northerners when she wrote the famous Battle Hymn of the Republic:

> In the beauty of the lilies Christ was born across the sea,
> With a glory in His bosom that transfigures you and me;
> As He died to make men holy, let us die to make men free!
> While God is marching on.
> Glory! Glory! Hallelujah!
> Glory! Glory! Hallelujah!
> Glory! Glory! Hallelujah!
> While God is marching on.

Less well known perhaps, but just as adamant, is the hymn written by Henry Timrod (1826-1867), of South Carolina, during the first meeting of the Confederate Congress. In this view, the North was warring with God. But, Timrod, exclaimed:

We shall not shrink, my brothers, but go forth
To meet them, marshalled by the Lord of Hosts. . .[12]

It cannot be said emphatically enough: God is not a partisan God, who supports one nation or one ethnic group or one political party or denomination and ignores or opposes other nations or groups. In World War II, God was not the God of the Germans, but neither was He the God of the Western Allies. Today, He is not the God of the Protestants in Northern Ireland rather than the God of the Catholics. He is not the God of the Croats, rather than the God of the Serbs. He is not the God of the Baptists, the Pentecostals, or even the Adventists. He is not the God of the conservatives nor of the liberals. He is not the God of the vegetarians nor of the meat eaters. God is not an idol who serves just one or two special-interest groups. The true God is the God of heaven and earth and the God of all mankind.

It may at times appear in the Old Testament that God acted in parochial ways and usually teamed up with just one nation—Israel. However, that is not the case. The Israelites received a special commission, with unique responsibilities and privileges, but they did not have God in their pocket.

The Bible leaves no doubt that God is the God of all the world. "God so loved *the world*!" (John 3:16, emphasis supplied). This was also the fervent belief of King Solomon. When the temple was completed, the king himself offered the dedicatory prayer. He asked God to listen just as intently to the prayers of the "foreigners" as to those of the Israelites (2 Chronicles 6:32, 33). Psalm 86 expresses the same beautiful truth: "*All the nations* You have made will come and worship before You, O Lord; they will bring glory to Your name. For You are great and do marvelous deeds; You alone are God" (verses 9, 10).

Any god who is restricted to one nation or special interest group is an idol!

### Will the Christian God please stand?

One more important point needs to be made before we can end this chapter. The fact that theologians talk and write about the Christian God does not guarantee that they worship the God of the Bible rather than some other god.

Whenever theologians espouse a theology in which the border between the infinite, non-material God and finite reality is blurred and in which God is somehow made identical with, or inseparable from, the universe—they describe an idol. Whenever theologians make God less than perfect, less than eternal, less than omnipresent and all-knowing, they have created an idol. Whenever believers, whether they are respectable Unitarians or unpopular Jehovah's Witnesses, short change God by denying His mysterious threeness-in-oneness, they do not worship the only true God and hence are guilty of idolatry!

The God of John Calvin, who leaves no room for human choice, is not the true God but an idol. The Calvinistic God, who has decreed from all eternity who will be saved and who will be lost, is not the loving Father of Jesus Christ who invites all men and women to come to Him. The biblical God wants us to make a conscious decision to serve Him. He gives us the same choice that Joshua presented to the people of Israel almost 3,500 years ago (just remember to substitute the modern idols we discussed earlier in this chapter for the idols of Joshua's time):

> Now fear the Lord and serve him with all faithfulness. Throw away the gods your forefathers worshiped beyond the River and in Egypt, and serve the Lord.
>
> But if serving the Lord seems undesirable to you, then choose for yourselves this day whom you will serve, whether the gods your forefathers served beyond the River, or the gods of the Amorites, in whose land you are living. But as for me and my household, we will serve the Lord (Joshua 24:14, 15).

Neither can we recognize the true God of the Bible in the god of many feminist theologians: In their zeal to eradicate any talk about God as our Father they often advocate the idea that God is our Great Mother.

In the process, they tend to introduce a long series of associations that are sub-Christian if not totally pagan.

Let me mention just one other example of false concepts of God being circulated today. There is something seriously wrong with the God of Robert Schuler and a range of other preachers who are presenting an attractive, but utterly false, health-and-wealth gospel. Of course, there are texts in the Bible that stress the importance of health and prosperity and the fact that God is able to bless abundantly. But in the Bible, Christianity and faith is more than "possibility thinking," and salvation is more than a change from a negative to a positive self-image. "The theology of self-esteem and the theology of prosperity," writes Baptist theologian David L. Smith, "were hatched in the incubator of the 'American dream' and are closely related to the visions of success and the concept of Manifest Destiny that have been so characteristic of American thinking." He goes on to state:

> Both of them suffer from severe deficiencies in their ideas of how God and humanity relate to one another. Both operate on the assumption that humans are entitled to well-being and happiness. But the Bible teaches that, because of sin, they are "entitled" to nothing except God's wrath. Anything good they receive is not the result of entitlement, but of God's free and unmerited grace. . . . Prosperity theology deifies humanity at God's expense.[13]

The conclusion to all this must be: Beware. The world is full of idols, of "strange" gods. Often they try to disguise themselves as the God of the Bible. We must know the difference between the myriad of idols and the one and only true Christian God. He is the heart of our religion. The core of the Christian faith is not the Sabbath, or healthful living, tithing or a correct understanding of the state of the dead, however important these things may be. The heart of all true Christian religion is the worship of the one and only true God!

To Him we now turn.

---

[1] Ellen G. White, *Spirit of Prophecy*, vol. 1, 34.
[2] Vinoth Ramachandra, *Gods that Fail* (Downers Grove, Ill.: InterVarsity Press, 1996), 19.
[3] Ellen G. White, *Selected Messages*, vol. 3, 330.
[4] Ellen G. White, *Great Controversy*, 583.
[5] Richard J. Foster, *Money, Sex and Power—the Challenge of a Disciplined Life* (London: Hodder and Stoughton, 1985), 25-31.
[6] Robert Wuthnow, *Rethinking Materialism—Perspectives on the Spiritual Dimension of Economic Behavior* (Grand Rapids, Mich.: William B. Eerdmans Publishing Company, 1995), 130.
[7] Ellen G. White, *The Faith I Live By*, 154.
[8] Wuthnow, 127.
[9] Ramachandra, 153, 171.
[10] Richard Rice, *The Reign of God* (Berrien Springs, Mich.: Andrews University Press, 1985), 71,72.
[11] Philip Schaff, *History of the Christian Church*, vol. V (William B. Eerdmans Publishing Company, 1907), 228ff.
[12] Mark A. Knoll, *A History of Christianity in the United States* (Grand Rapids, Mich.: William B. Eerdmans Publishing Company, 1992), 313, 314.
[13] David L. Smith, *A Handbook of Contemporary Theology* (Wheaton, Ill.: Victor Books, 1992), 200, 201.

**Chapter Five**

# "How Great Thou Art"

Suppose you found yourself in the middle of a dense, equatorial jungle among a recently discovered tribe of primitive hunter-gatherers that has never been in contact with the civilized world outside. Imagine, further, that you are an expert on linguistics and that after a year or two of intense listening and observation you finally master the basics of these people's language. Finally, you can start communicating with them. You can begin to tell them about the world you came from before you were parachuted into their remote village. Think of the magnitude of such a challenge!

How would you begin to describe the world of concrete buildings, asphalt roads, and shopping centers? How would you begin to explain such things as elevators, traffic lights, and computers? How would you tell these people about cars and airplanes, McDonald's restaurants and Jacuzzi whirlpool baths? Clearly, you would have an impossible task.

I remember visiting, about ten years ago, a pygmy village in Eastern Zaire (presently called the Republic of Kongo) and how I stayed there for the night, sleeping on banana leaves in a simple thatched structure. The villagers had seen a few white people before and were therefore not too shocked at my appearance. Monthly, a small mission plane landed on the narrow, somewhat crooked and bumpy, airstrip about five miles from the village to provide the people with basic medical and dental care. A few years earlier, the villagers had become members of the Seventh-day Adventist Church. Since I was accompanied by an interpreter, I was invited to preach. But I must admit that the further I got in my sermon, the more uncomfortable I felt as I looked at the eighty or ninety faces radiating a curious mixture of sublime friendliness and total incomprehension.

It was quite clear to me that I did not get through that morning to my vertically-challenged sisters and brothers. I came from another world, and most of what I said was utterly meaningless to them. Explaining the things I was familiar with to these people, whose world was confined to a small section of the African rain forest, proved to be a greater challenge than I could handle successfully.

Yet, the distance between God's world and ours is far greater than the distance separating my world from that of the pygmies or the distance between our imaginary linguist and a recently discovered tribe. But if there is such an immense distance between God and me, how can I ever hope to comprehend Him or even to find words to describe Him?

I do not have those words nor can I form any kind of mental picture that would help me to communicate fully what God is like. It has been rightly said: "Trying to define God is like trying to put the ocean in a hole dug on the beach."[1] It is totally beyond us.

Nonetheless, through the centuries, great philosophers have tried to put their concepts of God into human language—that is to say, into a jargon that some who are trained in philosophy can understand, but that remains largely abracadabra to those who have not been initiated into that discipline. Many have built on the work of the famous medieval philosopher and theologian Thomas Aquinas (1225-1274) and have followed him in concluding that it is actually easier to describe what God *is not* than to say what He *is*. These philosophers invariably insist that if God exists, He must be in a totally unique category, all by Himself, incomparable to anything or anyone else.

To further complicate matters, many have disputed whether it would even be a proper use of language to say that God "exists." Those philosophers who do support the idea that God "exists" usually stress that He does not "exist" in the same way as all other things and beings exist. He is not an object among other objects or a being among other beings. In fact, if He is to be the real God, He must be nonmaterial and nonspatial. Being God, He is not made of some substance, however ethereal, nor is He confined to a particular space, however distant or palatial. "God is a Spirit," the apostle John quotes Jesus as saying, "and they that worship Him must worship Him in spirit and in truth" (John 4:24).

### Infinity

In this chapter, and particularly in the following two chapters, we will be looking in more detail at the biblical evidence about God. As we do so, we must first emphasize—and we cannot emphasize it enough—that God is infinite. "Great is the Lord, and greatly to be praised; and his greatness is unsearchable" (Psalm 145:3).

*Over and against finite objects and finite beings is the One who is the Infinite.* That statement seems to be sound enough, but what does it really mean?

We know what it means to be finite, to be limited in power and knowledge and to be confined in our ambitions and achievements by the resources that are at our disposal and by time and space. We may dream of having more power, more resources, and more knowledge; we may even be able to imagine what it could mean to live two hundred years and to travel by rocket to Australia in thirty minutes, but we soon reach the limits of our imaginations. To be infinite is so far removed from us that the word is almost meaningless.

Let us, nonetheless, probe the concept of infinity for a few moments. At the moment that I am writing these sentences, Bill Gates, chairman of the Microsoft Corporation, is reputed to be the richest man on earth with an estimated total net worth of approximately $80 billion. That is a lot of money by any definition! To me, such riches seem infinite. How could one ever spend so much money? If you live 80 years, that gives you roughly 30,000 days on this planet. You would have to spend almost $3 million each and every day, seven days a week, from the day of your birth till the day you died to go through $80 billion. But even that would not make you poor, for you would receive income from investments and interest payments. It does not take great mathematical talent to work out that the interest on $80 billion might easily reach $10 million or so a day! Or to look at it from another angle: How many $20,000 automobiles would you be able to buy if you were as rich as Bill Gates? The answer is four million! I would imagine, however, that you might be able to negotiate a healthy discount if you were to buy in that kind of bulk, and so the number would go up considerably.

God is incomparably richer, however, than Bill Gates. He owns everything; as the poet who wrote Psalm 50 so vividly expressed it: "He owns all the cattle on a thousand hills!" (see verse 10). Bill Gates's wealth may look infinite to those of us who earn an average salary and struggle to make our mortgage payments, but it *is* finite! It is nothing compared to what God owns.

Let's take another example that is even more mind boggling. I could not believe it when I first read it, but I have checked a number of sources and have found confirmation. If you are a chess player, you know that a chess board is made up of sixty-four squares and that each player has sixteen pieces at his disposal. For the first move, the players are restricted to a few possibilities—they can move their pawns one or two squares forward or they can move their knights. After this first move, the players then have four hundred possible moves from which to choose. After two moves, the possibilities have increased to 71,852, and after three moves to an incredible 9 million choices! The number of possible different moves in a forty-move game is 25 times 10 to the $155^{\text{th}}$ power, or

25,000,000,000,000,000,000,000,000,000,000,000,000,000,000,000,000
000,000,000,000,000,000,000,000,000,000,000,000,000,000,000,000
000,000,000,000,000,000,000,000,000,000,000,000,000,000,000,000,
000,000,000,000,000,000,000.[2]

No wonder no game of chess is ever the same!

Is this infinity? No, it is just a very large number. It is nothing compared to the possible "moves" the infinite God can choose. Jesus Christ confirmed this when He said, " 'With God all things are possible' " (Matthew 19:26).

Infinity is closely linked to the concept of eternity. Scientists who support the theory of evolution tell us that we must go back hundreds of millions of years to arrive at the point in time when the first forms of primitive life originated. They insist that evolution simply takes time—a lot of time. And also that, eventually, after many millions of years, life as we now know it will once again become extinct and this planet of ours will finally cease to exist. All this may seem to us as taking an eternity. But a few hundred million years is something quite different from infinite time. It is a very long period, but real eternity is something else. The eternity of God ("the King eternal, immortal, invisible" 1 Timothy 1:17) is incomparable to any kind of "eternities" we can think of in daily life; He is incomparable even to the "eternities" to which the evolutionists like to refer.

### God is everywhere

So God is infinite—whatever that means—in terms of the options He can choose, in terms of what He possesses, and in terms of time. But He is also infinite in terms of space. He is omnipresent, that is, He is everywhere at the same time. He fills the universe. Jeremiah echoes God's question: " 'Can any hide himself in secret places that I shall not see him? . . . Do not I fill heaven and earth?' " (Jeremiah 23: 24).

As the centuries have passed, we have gradually realized that the universe is always larger than we dare to think. Of course, the concept of a "universe" is, itself, difficult to fathom. How can there not be an end to the universe? If there were an outer limit, however, what would there be beyond those distant borders?

It took a while, but humanity eventually learned that the earth does not hold center stage in the universe. In fact, the earth is no more than an insignificant speck of dust compared to other heavenly bodies. One million earths could comfortably fit in the volume of the sun! As we now know, the sun is just one of a great number of stars. How many stars are there in the universe? My reading tells me there are some one hundred thousand million stars in the Milky Way galaxy alone and that there may be as many as one hundred thousand million galaxies in the universe! My pocket calculator refuses to provide the answer; the little glass window is too small. I will therefore have to calculate it on paper. The number of stars in the universe is at least:

100,000,000,000 x 100,000,000,000
= 10,000,000,000,000,000,000,000.[3]

Thinkers in ancient Greece concluded that the moon is approximately sixty earth-radii distant from the earth and that the sun is about nineteen times farther from the earth than is the moon. According to Ptolemy (c. 100 - c. 170), the distance from the earth to the outer parts of the sky is some 20,000 earth radii. That would give the universe a diameter of approximately 140 million kilometers. Nicolaus Copernicus (1473-1543) later suggested that the universe was some 200 times bigger than the ancient Greeks had estimated. The famous Dutch astronomer Jacobus Cornelius Kapteyn (1851-1922) revised even these figures sharply upwards. The Milky Way galaxy alone, he said, was about 300,000,000,000,000,000 kilometers in diameter, or about 30,000 light years. Hubble (1889-1953), whose name is more familiar to us since being attached to the Hubble Space Telescope, the largest telescope in space, concluded that the universe has a diameter of no less than a million light years, that is to say:

10,000,000,000,000,000,000 kilometers.[4]

Modern astronomy has once again enlarged our universe. It is now quite generally accepted that the universe has a diameter of some fifteen thousand million light years, or

150,000,000,000,000,000,000,000 kilometers.

On the other hand, modern measurement techniques also make it possible to meet near-infinity in the other direction by helping us to measure, ever more precisely, the tiniest things both in space and time. We are no longer content to measure objects in centimeters or millimeters. Using lasers, nanotechnology helps us to determine distances the size of an atom—one ten-millionth of a millimeter. (If you want to be meticulous about it, you may want to double check the definition of a millimeter; a millimeter is one-thousandth of the distance traveled by light in a vacuum in 1/299,792,458 of a second!)

I am reminded of the words of the German novelist Thomas Mann (1875-1955):

> The data of the cosmos are like an anesthetic bombardment on our intelligence, with numbers that have comet tails of two dozen zeros and pretend that they have any relationship to measurement and comprehension.[5]

All this should make us rather humble. Who are we humans? If the entire population of the earth were dumped in the Lake of Constanz in Switzerland, the water level would rise no more than about one inch![6]

When we say that God is omnipresent—that He is everywhere at the same time—we are saying that He is in the smallest possible particle and also that He is everywhere in the ever-expanding universe! We have every reason to sing that beautiful song, "How Great Thou Art," when we "consider . . .in awesome wonder . . .[God's] power throughout the universe displayed!"[7]

**He knows everything and can do anything**

If God is infinite, this must apply also to His knowledge and to His power. Infinity in terms of these aspects is just as difficult to grasp as is the fact that He is not limited in space or time.

# "How Great Thou Art"

Some people seem to have an incredible knowledge of a wide range of subjects and an almost infinite knowledge in their particular specialty. Anyone familiar with *Jeopardy* or similar television quiz shows will wonder at times how some people can know so much about certain subjects.

The amount of knowledge presently available is staggering. A high school student today may know more than a medieval top-scholar could ever have hoped to know. And the body of available knowledge increases constantly and exponentially. University libraries contain hundreds of thousands, or even millions, of books. The Internet is a relatively new research tool that shows how much knowledge mankind has amassed! But God knows more. "Known unto God are all his works from the beginning of the world"(Acts 15:18, KJV). "He determines the number of the stars and calls them each by name. Great is our Lord and mighty in power: his understanding has no limit" (Psalm 147:4, 5).

All the information stored in the libraries around the globe and entrusted to all the computers in the world is nothing compared to what God knows. For He knows not only all that, but He also knows what people knew in ancient times that has remained unrecorded. He also knows everything that goes on in human brains, even when it is never put into speech or writing. He also knows of all the inventions scientists are presently working on and about all the things we and our descendants will yet do! It is mind-boggling, indeed.

And the same is true with regard to God's power. Human beings have invented powerful tools; consider, for example, the terrifying forces that are unleashed in nuclear explosions. Even this kind of physical power is mere child's play compared to God's infinite, omnipotent, power.

Through the centuries, some men and women have had almost limitless power. Think of men (yes, they were mostly men!) such as Alexander the Great, Nero, Charlemagne, or more recently, Hitler and Stalin. Dictators such as Idi Amin and Bokassa have been able to indulge in a reign of terror and do whatever took their fancy. Presidents and prime ministers of major countries have great influence. Often it is their prerogative to grant a pardon or to send combat troops into war, thus deciding the life and death of thousands. But all the power of tyrants, dictators, kings, emperors, presidents, and ministers combined is nothing compared to the infinite power of God.

**But beware. . .**

Any attempt to say something meaningful about our awesome God needs to begin with this basic notion—God is infinite, unlimited, not bound by space or time, beyond everything we can possibly imagine. This fundamental fact sets us on the right path as we try to search—in nature, but primarily in the Bible—for further clues of what God is like. Whatever we find must be considered against the backdrop of His infinity. When we think we have grasped something about His attributes, we must bow down and remember that whatever we have found is only a human way of speaking about a God who is infinitely greater than any thought we can think. Remembering that God is infinite will help us to maintain the right perspective.

We can end up with a false concept of God if our view of His infinity is defective. Throughout the centuries, most people have concluded that there must be a God. But they also saw evil, death and destruction, misery and madness, and they have posed the age-old question: How can a God who is so infinite in knowledge and power apparently be so unwilling or unable to deal with the mess that we see around us? Many have concluded that God exists, but that He does not get actively involved with the world and its inhabitants. People who adopt this view are called "deists." They believe in God, but see Him as being in a state of retirement or, at least, semi-retirement. He is there; He is infinite in power, but has simply chosen not to use it.

It may not be easy to reconcile trust in God with the horrific reality of evil, but the "deist model" is far from satisfying, and it is unbiblical. The same is true for the approach some modern "process theologians" have adopted. The ideas of "process-theology" and the philosophical presuppositions on which they are built are not easily expressed in popular language. They boil down to the theory that God can be said to be infinite in power only in comparison to our human limitations, that He is suffering with us when things go wrong because of the choices we make, individually and collectively, and that He is learning as He goes along.

The question of why bad things happen to good people[8] is a difficult one, but the answers of the "deists" and the "process-theologians" cannot be right since they fail to do justice to the biblical notion that God is infinite. And God would be just a god—not God—if He were less than infinite.

There is yet another, possibly more frequent, misconception about God that is also based on a one-sided view of His infinite greatness—pantheism, or its modern derivative, panentheism. Pantheists believe that God is everywhere, in everything that exists. So far so good; that is orthodox teaching. But they continue to assert that, in actual fact, God is *equal to* everything and, thus, that everything *is* God. God is not a Person (a notion we will return to in a later chapter) who exists in His own right, but He is the sum total of all that exists. This means that God is not above and beyond nature, but that He *is* nature. The trees, the oceans, the mountains are God. Panentheists do not go quite as far and do not believe in a total merger of God and matter. They more or less see God as an extra, spiritual dimension of all that is; therefore their concept of God also falls far short of the Christian (biblical) concept of the Most High.[9]

In the Christian concept of God, His infinity forms the basis upon which other significant statements about Him can be made—statements about His personhood and, in particular, about His love. Without these basic notions, an emphasis on God's infinity will lead us astray. But without a true sense of our own smallness and God's infinite greatness, we will soon lose sight of heavenly realities and will be constantly tempted to make a god in our own image.

---

[1] Gene Edward Veith Jr., *Postmodern Times: A Christian Guide to Contemporary Thought and Culture* (Wheaton, Ill: Crossway Books, 1994), 69.

[2] Martin E. Marty, 'Voices of Theologians and Humanists', in: John Marks Templeton, ed., *How Large is God? Voices of Scientists and Theologians* (Philadelphia: Templeton Foundations

Press, 1997), 197f.

[3] F. Russell Stannard, 'Approaching God Through Paradox', in: Templeton, *op. cit.*, 81.

[4] Owen Gingerich, 'An Astronomical Perspective, in: Templeton, *op cit.*, 24-34.

[5] Quoted in: Okke Jager, *Oude Beelden Spreken een Nieuwe Taal - Geloven na de Geloofscrisis* (Baarn: Ten Have, 1990), 47.

[6] *Ibid.*, 49.

[7] Hymn 86 in the *Seventh-day Adventist Hymnal* (Hagerstown, Md.: Review and Herald Publishing Association, 1985).

[8] Cf. the title of the best-seller by Harold Kushner, *When Bad Things Happen to Good People* (New York: Schocken Books, 1981).

[9] For an insightful critique of this trend by an outstanding evangelical scholar, see Norman L. Geisler, *Creating God in the Image of Man* (Minneapolis, Minn.: Bethany House Publishers, 1997).

**Chapter Six**

# God Has a Name

Pablo Picasso (1881-1973), the eccentric Spanish artist, was not impressed by those who claimed they could clearly see the hand of God in nature around them. "God is really just another artist," Picasso is reported to have said. "He invented the giraffe, the elephant, and the cat. He has no real style. He just keeps on trying other things."[1]

It may have been abundantly clear to the author of Psalm 19 that "the heavens declare the glory of God" (verse 1), but Clifford Stoll, a Christian astronomer known for his research in Jupiter's atmosphere and best-selling author, writes: "As an astronomer, I watch the heavens, but am no closer to the Creator than a physician to your soul."[2] On the other hand, Chris Erickson, from Nebraska, who works on the farm that has been in his family for over a century, is adamant that he sees God every day as he goes about his tasks in the fields. "I cannot think of one occupation," he says, "outside the clergy that would expose a person to God and His creation more than farming." He tells about the many hours spent planting the seeds, tilling the fields, watering the crops, and harvesting the grain. "But I have nothing to do with the seeds sprouting or the plants growing," he says. "When I see all this, I experience God's creation."[3]

# OUR AWESOME GOD

Does nature reveal at least something of the Christian God? Or do we have to look elsewhere? "Yes," affirms Ellen G. White, "nature does tell us about God." "Nature and revelation alike testify of God's love."[4] "Yes," also reply most of the theologians of the past and the present. But they usually emphasize that nature provides only a "general" kind of revelation, and they differ sharply on *how much* nature can reveal of God's essence. They usually refer to a few passages of Scripture that do indeed point in the direction of a "general" revelation through nature.

In addition to Psalm 19, already quoted above, other psalms affirm that nature points beyond itself to the great Creator God. Read, for instance, Psalm 8: "When I consider Your heavens, the work of Your fingers, the moon and the stars, which You have set in place . . . O Lord, our Lord, how majestic is Your name in all the earth!" (verses 3, 8). And take a Bible from your bookshelf and read Psalm 104 and Psalm 148.

Some New Testament texts make the same point—that God reveals at least something of Himself in nature. When rebuking the people of Lystra in Asia Minor for their lack of spiritual understanding, the apostle Paul makes the remarkable statement that God "has not left Himself without testimony: He has shown kindness by giving you rain from heaven and crops in their seasons; He provides you with plenty of food and fills your hearts with joy" (Acts 14:17). In other words, God did something the Lystrans should have recognized as coming from a greater power than that possessed by any of their gods. Paul made very much the same point when, somewhat later, he argued and pled with the Athenians (see Acts 17:22-31).

But, no doubt, the most famous text on this subject is Romans 1:20: "For since the creation of the world God's invisible qualities—His eternal power and divine nature—have been clearly seen, being understood from what has been made, so that men are without excuse." This is indeed a powerful statement. It led Jimmy Carter, a former United States president, to remark, "If Paul expected the ancient Romans to believe in God because of their relatively limited observations of the world around them, shouldn't our faith be stronger, since we know so much more?"[5]

So, we acknowledge that nature points beyond itself to something higher, or even to Someone higher. People may have a valid excuse for not knowing precisely what God has done for them in Jesus Christ, but they have no excuse for not having a sense of something or Someone beyond. Their experience may not be quite as exuberant and distinct as that of the famous eighteenth-century preacher and theologian, Jonathan Edwards, who looking at the sky and the clouds, had a miraculous sensation of God's majesty and grace that was so intense he did not know how to express it in words,[6] but nature should provide them with some basic spiritual insight.

This insight that nature gives us of God does, however, have its severe limitations. Because of the enormous distance between God and man, and because of the terrible disturbance sin has created, humans cannot get a clear picture of God through nature. Nature can be very beautiful and, at times, fill us with awe and rapture, but as we watch the nature films on the Discovery channel or look at the pictures in the *National Geographic* as we sit in the dentist's waiting room, we can also see plenty of horrific cruelty and senseless waste in nature. For once, we Christians can agree with Charles Darwin, when he wrote to Asa Gray:

> There seems to me so much misery in the world. I cannot persuade myself that a beneficent and omnipotent God would have designedly created the Ichneumonidae with their express intention of their feeding within the living bodies of Caterpillars, or that a cat should play with mice.[7]

Those who have read the first chapters of the Bible, however, know the reason for these disturbing aspects of nature—every part of God's beautiful world has been affected by the regrettable introduction of evil on planet Earth. Yet, Ellen White ranks God's artistry considerably higher than either Picasso or Darwin were willing to do:

> The things of nature upon which we look today give us but a faint conception of Eden's beauty and glory. Yet much that is

> beautiful remains. Nature testifies that One infinite in power, great in goodness, mercy, and love, created the earth and filled it with life and gladness. Even in their blighted state all things reveal the handiwork of the great Master Artist.[8]

We should also take a brief look at another possible avenue of gaining some basic knowledge about God. It has been argued that God not only reveals Himself in nature, but also in history. If you look at the way in which history moves forward, you can catch glimpses of a divine power that steers the affairs of mankind. But this idea has, I fear, far more problems than those posed by a "general" revelation of God through nature. Sin has left an even more deadly imprint on the history of peoples and nations than it has on nature.

It would probably be accurate to say that to those who are able to look with eyes of faith, God's hand is visible in the affairs of mankind. It took some very drastic divine measures before the Babylonian king Nebuchadnezzar, for instance, was able to see with eyes of faith and was willing to acknowledge that God indeed "lives forever" and that "His dominion is an eternal dominion" and that "His kingdom endures from generation to generation" (Daniel 4:34). It took him seven years to come to that realization. Those who have already come to believe in God may, like the ancient monarch, see a confirmation of His presence in the world by their study of past and contemporary events. But history usually does not reveal much about God to those who can see only with physical eyes and not with the sight of faith.

Natural theology—the branch of theology that searches for information about God in sources outside the Bible—can at best provide us with a distorted or a limited view of who and what God is. If we want to know more, we need an additional, less "general," kind of revelation.[9]

### God reveals Himself in His Word

For a fuller revelation of who and what God is, we must turn to the Bible, the Word of God. Even here, however, we will soon realize, as we begin reading the Scriptures, that it does not present us with any systematic, philosophical statement about the nature and attributes of God. Yet, somehow the picture of God grows on us, as we continue to spend time with His Word.

There is nothing wrong with using the conceptual language of philosophy when we think about God. But we must always remind ourselves that God cannot be reduced to the axioms of logic or to an object of our understanding. And we must always acknowledge that while we may arrive at some true knowledge of God, that knowledge will always be only partial. Some mystics would go as far as to say that God can be experienced only and that He is totally unknowable in any other way. That, fortunately, is not true. God's self-revelation in His Word allows us to know Him, although "in part" (1 Corinthians 13:9).

Even utilizing all the avenues we have to gain a knowledge of God, many aspects about Him will remain a mystery to us. Theologians have often stressed that God is simultaneously a revealed God (*Deus revelatus*) and a hidden God (*Deus absconditus*). Some well-known Bible texts illustrate God's hiddenness. Deuteronomy 29:29 is the classic statement about the polarity between His being revealed and His remaining hidden: "The secret things belong to the Lord our God, but the things revealed belong to us and to our children forever." The prophet Isaiah realized that God must remain hidden, since mortal man cannot survive a direct exposure to His full glory (see Isaiah 6:5).

The infinite distance between humans and God prevents a full revelation of Him, but the revelation we have is adequate for our human needs. We will never comprehend Him, but we may begin to understand His love for us and His plan for our lives. Drawing on the figurative language of the poetic sections of the Bible and the biblical narratives in which God is the main Player, we can "abound more and more in knowledge and depth of insight" (Philippians 1:9).

The Bible describes God through different metaphors. Each contributes to a fuller understanding of who and what He is. God is often referred to as "King" (e.g. Psalm 10:16; 47:6), but He is also called a Warrior "mighty in battle"(e.g. Psalm 24:8) and a "Shepherd" (e.g. Psalm 23). We would have a hard time finding a human being, who at one and the same time combines these three activities. We know of King David, who was a shepherd before he became king and was a warrior both before and after he ascended to the throne. But he was never all three at the same time. Being both a warrior and a shepherd are activities that can hardly be combined, humanly speaking, but in the realm of the divine these metaphors do not contradict each other; rather, they complement each other. God is King; He is the Sovereign Lord who rules with majesty and splendor. At the same time, He is also the Warrior who will fight any battle for His subjects and who ensures their victory. Yet, His majesty and strength do not in any way diminish his wonderful, unparalleled compassion. The One who is "the Lord, your Holy One, Israel's Creator, your King" (Isaiah 43:15) is also the Shepherd who guarantees that we "shall not be in want", and who leads us "beside quiet waters," restores our soul and guides us "in paths of righteousness for His name's sake' " (Psalm 23:1-3).

**Can God change?**

In the previous chapter we already noted that the God of the Bible is infinite, omnipotent (almighty), and omniscient (all-knowing). This implies that He is perfect. We now need to take this concept a little further. Through the centuries, philosophers and theologians have argued about whether the fact that God is perfect also means that He cannot change. The argument runs like this: If God is perfect, then any change from His perfection would make Him imperfect. Thus God cannot change. We cannot solve the matter simply by quoting the well-known text from James's letter referring to God as "the Father of the heavenly lights, who *does not change* like shifting shadows" (1:17, emphasis supplied). For other texts can be quoted that suggest that God can at least change His mind. Think of God's dealings with the city of Nineveh in Jonah's day. God's message to the inhabitants of that ancient metropolis, in what is today northern Iraq, declared that they faced imminent destruction. But when the Ninevites repented and God "saw what they did and how they turned from their evil ways, He had compassion and did not bring upon them the destruction He had threatened" (Jonah 3:10). God apparently changed His mind, and this was not the only time He did so. Of course, we could simply say that this example does not really prove that God can change, it just indicates how constant and unchanging He is in His love!

The issue is, however, even more complicated. What is at stake is the question: Can God have emotions? Can He feel pain? Can He suffer? Or is He impassible (a technical term meaning "unable to suffer")? If God has emotions, it implies that He is subject to change. And any change would, of necessity, make Him either more perfect or less perfect than He was before the change. But how can it possibly be said that God could become less perfect or more perfect if we believe that He was, is, and ever shall be "perfectly perfect?"

Once again, we must realize that logic alone will not suffice if we want to know more about God. Of course, we must accept that God does not have emotions in the same way as we have. And we must further accept that God suffered in a totally unique way in His Son Jesus Christ. Through the incarnation of Jesus, God shared in our human predicament, with all the accompanying emotions, in a more profound way than we can ever imagine.

The German theologian Jürgen Moltmann (1926- ), who after Karl Barth may well be the best-known Reformed theologian of the twentieth century, makes an important point when he states that a God who is unable to suffer cannot be perfect. Such a God would be poorer than a human being; He would be a being who cannot be engaged![10] We may not be able to give a good philosophical answer to the question of how a perfect God can suffer and even experience death, but with Charles Wesley we can, nonetheless, sing:

> Amazing love! How can it be?
> That Thou, my God, shouldst die for me?[11]

### A holy God and a loving God

When asked what the word "holy" means, most people will come up with terms such as "sinless," "good," "superior," "supernatural," or "virtuous." And, indeed, all these shades of meaning, and more, would apply. Many people, on the other hand, might also be inclined to attach some negative feelings to holiness. We do not always like "holy people;" in fact, we tend to get irritated when people are very "holy" in the way they talk, especially when there is a discrepancy between what they do and what they say.

In the Bible the word "holy" refers to what is good and honorable, but its root meaning is separation from all that is unclean and from everything that is of mere passing significance. A plot of land, a mountain, or a building can be holy. Utensils, garments, and many other objects can be holy. People who are in God's service are supposed to be holy. In all these cases the basic idea is that these objects or persons are separate from everyday use or normal activities; they are set apart from what is ordinary and profane. They are in a special class for a special, higher, purpose. And this is precisely what we want to say about our God when we say that He is "holy;" He is in a special class all by Himself!

Hundreds of times the Bible refers to God as the "Holy One" (e.g. Proverbs 9:10; Hosea 11:9; 1 John 2:20, etc.). Isaiah 40:25 employs the same term when the prophet quotes the divine question: " 'To whom will you compare Me? Or who is My equal?' says the Holy One." In other texts, God is referred to as "the Holy One of Israel" (e.g. Isaiah 1:4; 5:19, 24; 41:14; 43:14, etc.) or is acclaimed as "majestic in holiness" (e.g. Exodus 15:11). The angels sing "Holy, holy, holy" (Revelation 4:8), and Jesus calls God the " 'Holy Father' " (John 17:11) and teaches us to pray that God's name be " 'hallowed' " (Matthew 6:9) or made holy.

Another attribute of God is His love. Here we touch on His very nature. "Whoever does not love does not know God, because God is love . . . And so we know and rely on the love God has for us. God is love" (1 John 4:8, 16). This love has no match anywhere in the universe:

> Neither death nor life, neither angels nor demons, neither the present nor the future, nor any powers, neither height nor depth, nor anything else in all creation, will be able to separate

> us from the love of God that is in Christ Jesus our Lord (Romans 8:38, 39).

We should never confuse this divine love with what the world around us calls "love." The best way to contrast the radical difference between divine love and human love is by looking at the dissimilarity between the Greek concepts of *eros*-love and *agape*-love. The word "eros," from which the English word "erotic" is derived, does not occur in the New Testament, yet it is helpful to refer to it by way of contrast. The word "agape" occurs many times in the New Testament as the description for the totally selfless love that God has for His creatures. The meaning of "eros" is richer than sexual love, although that aspect definitely can be a very positive and integral part of human love. The basic difference between human *eros*-love and divine *agape*-love is that the former is usually based on a desire to posses and to enjoy, whereas *agape*-love is characterized by its willingness to serve without reservations. *Eros* is attracted to that which has the greatest value; *agape* goes out to the least worthy. *Eros* discovers value, whereas *agape* creates value. Human love may inspire us to use power in the right way, whereas *agape*-love is willing to surrender power and triumphs through powerlessness. *Eros* is a need-love, but *agape* is a gift-love.

The supreme revelation of *agape* is God's self-condescension in Jesus Christ. And of course, it is this *agape*-love that the true Christian is challenged to emulate.[12]

The love Christians are to demonstrate should not be confused with humanitarianism. It goes far beyond that. "Humanitarianism lends a helping hand to the deprived and the forsaken; *agape* vicariously identifies with the castaways of society."[13]

God is holy, and God is love. These two sublime aspects of His nature must be kept together as the two sides of the biblical God. Evangelical theologian Donald G. Bloesch is worth quoting at this point:

> Biblical faith portrays God as having two sides: holiness and love. These are the perfections that shape the interaction of God with His

> people. They are integrally related, and yet they coexist in a certain tension, one that highlights their paradoxical unity rather than dissolves it. God's holiness is His majestic purity that cannot tolerate moral evil. God's love is His outgoing, tenderhearted embrace of the sinner. God's holiness is His separateness from what is unclean and profane. God's love is His willingness to identify with those who are unclean in order to help them. God's holiness transcends the passing world of decay and death. God's love incarnates itself in this world corrupted by sin.[14]

Few could have said it better! But even though the concepts of holiness and love are foundational to any real understanding of the character of God, other aspects must also be related to these two attributes. The Bible speaks, for instance, about God's anger and even His jealousy. It speaks of His wrath and His "strange" acts of punishments (His "alien task," Isaiah 28:21).

God loves mankind, but He is also the lawgiver and ruler. It is important that all these aspects of God's nature are understood within the framework of His infinite love. If He is jealous and does not want us to follow other gods, it is for *our* sake. If He is wrathful, it is not because He has occasional, uncontrollable fits of anger like we tend to have, but because His wrath is the corollary of His holiness that must ultimately annihilate what is unclean. If God demands that we keep His law, it is because the law reflects His character and He wants us to be guided by its principles so that we can live fulfilled lives.

When God wanted to reveal Himself to Moses, He issued a basic statement of who He is. We find it in Exodus 34:6, 7:

> "The Lord, the Lord, the compassionate and gracious God, slow to anger, abounding in love and faithfulness, maintaining love to thousands, and forgiving wickedness, rebellion and sin. Yet He does not leave the guilty unpunished; He punishes the children and their children for the sin of the fathers to the third and fourth generation" (Exodus 34:6, 7).

# God Has a Name

It can hardly escape us how beautifully the various attributes are balanced. Love, grace and mercy, perfectly balanced by righteousness, justice and love. Unfortunately, most of our English translations do not do full justice to this statement. The text says that God maintains His love "to thousands." It should, in fact, read: "to thousands of generations." Notice the contrast with the assurance that God's punishment does not extend beyond "the third and fourth generation."[15]

> The Lord is compassionate and gracious, slow to anger, abounding in love.
>
> He will not always accuse, nor will He harbor His anger forever;
>
> He does not treat us as our sins deserve or repay us according to our iniquities.
>
> For as high as the heavens are above the earth, so great is His love for those who fear Him; as far as the east is from the west, so far has He removed our transgressions from us.
>
> As a father has compassion on his children, so the Lord has compassion on those who fear Him (Psalm 103:8-13).

**God has a name**

To most of us, names are relatively unimportant. What's in a name? But not so for the people in Bible times! They believed there was a vital connection between the name and the person it identified; a name somehow represented the nature of the person. At times, children would get an extraordinary name, directly related to the circumstances of the parents. But who today, even in the state of Israel, would call his son Mahershalalhashbaz, meaning "speed the spoil, hasten the prey," as Isaiah did when his country was threatened by an Assyrian invasion (Isaiah 8:3, 4)? Sometimes people of Bible times received a new name after they had gone through a life-changing experience; Abram became Abraham, for example; Jacob was later called Israel; and Saul became Paul!

Likewise, in the New Testament we find many indications that names were important. Jesus taught His disciples to pray to the Father saying,

'Hallowed be Your name' " (Matthew 6:9). Another striking illustration of the importance of the name is found in Acts 4:12: "There is no other name under heaven given to men by which we must be saved."

Therefore, it should not come as a surprise that God has a name, or that, as a matter of fact, He has several names! The word "God" is not a proper name but a generic substantive. It corresponds to the Hebrew "El" and its plural form "Elohim" which are used some 200 and 2,500 times respectively, in the Old Testament, and with the Greek word "theos," which gave us the English word "theology." The word "El" can be used by itself, but often it is connected with some other term and in the process becomes a proper name. God then becomes the El-Roi, the God who sees (Genesis 16:13), or El-Shaddai, the God Almighty. This latter name suggests "the abundant graciousness of God, the spiritual and temporal bounties with which God enriches His people."[16] In addition, the term "Adonai" is quite often used as a name for God when His sovereignty and lordship are being stressed.

The personal name of God *par excellence* is first encountered in Exodus 3 in the story of the burning bush. When God calls Moses to represent Him before the Egyptian Pharaoh, Moses is far from eager to accept the assignment. How the story then develops is clear from the following short passage:

> But Moses said to God, "Who am I, that I should go to Pharaoh and bring the Israelites out of Egypt?" And God said, "I will be with you. And this will be the sign to you that it is I who have sent you: When you have brought the people out of Egypt, you will worship God on this mountain."
>
> Moses said to God, "Suppose I go to the Israelites and say to them, 'The God of your fathers has sent me to you,' and they ask me, 'What is his name?' Then what shall I tell them?"
>
> God said to Moses, "I AM WHO I AM. This is what you are to say to the Israelites: 'I AM has sent me to you.' "
>
> God also said to Moses, "Say to the Israelites, 'The Lord, the

> God of your fathers—the God of Abraham, the God of Isaac and the God of Jacob—has sent me to you.' This is My name forever, the name by which I am to be remembered from generation to generation" (verses 11-15).

Reading the story, our first inclination may well be: What kind of non-answer is this? Moses desperately wants to know whom He must represent. He pleads, "Please, God, tell me Your name. Give me Your business card, with Your full name and address, so that I know where I can reach you when I have any questions."

"Sure," God says, "My name is simple, I AM WHO I AM, or, for my friends, simply, I AM."

In his commentary on Exodus, Old Testament scholar Jon Dybdahl assures us that God was not trying to be clever with words or evasive. God was serious with Moses. This was not a time for playing games; there was too much at stake. It is important for us to understand that "I am who I am" is not meant as a statement about God's essence or being, nor as a philosophical statement about God's preexistence or eternity. God identifies Himself by using a Hebrew verb, usually translated as "to be" or "to become," which would be translated in English as a continuous and future tense.[17] By identifying Himself through these words, God is saying, "I am here for you. I am with you. I protect you. You are never alone. You can count on Me—now, but also in the future: I will always be there for you!"

The name, Jahweh, used more than 5,000 times in the Bible, is based on this same verb found in Exodus 3:14. Because the written Hebrew language originally used only consonants, the name was spelled as JHWH—just four letters, referred to as the "tetragrammenon." This was eventually transformed into "Jehovah" through a curious set of circumstances. Because of their profound respect for God's holy name, His people in Old Testament times would not say "Jahweh" aloud. Instead, when they came to His name in Scripture, they would substitute *Adonai* (Lord), a practice still used today in the synagogue. In the Middle Ages, when vowels were added to the Hebrew consonants, the vowels of Adonai were attached to the consonants of JHWH, and the word "Jehovah" resulted.

By calling Himself the I AM, our holy and loving God is telling us, "I am everything the universe needs; I am everything you need. I am, to use Tillich's famous expression, the 'Ground of Being,' on which everything else depends." Compare that for a moment to what we human beings can say about ourselves. We are all kinds of things, but always in a very limited sense. I am a man, but what kind of a man am I? I am a church leader, but what kind of a leader am I? I am a husband and a father, but what kind of a husband or father am I? Whatever I think I am, and whatever you think you are, must always be qualified in a thousand ways. Not so with God. He is, and He will be there for us, in every possible way, now and forever more.

---

[1] Quoted in: Francoise Gilot and Carlton Lake, *Life with Picasso*, (London, Virago Press,1998),43.
[2] James Martin, ed., *How Can I Find God?* (Liguori, Missouri: Triumph Books, 1997), 20.
[3] *Ibid.*, 5,6.
[4] Ellen G. White, *Steps to Christ*, 9.
[5] Jimmy Carter, *Living Faith* (New York: Random House, 1996), 31.
[6] Jonathan Edwards, *Personal Narrative* in: Harold P. Simonson, *Selected Writings of Jonathan Edwards* (New York: F. Ungar Publ. Co, 1970), 31.
[7] Quoted in: Edwin J. Larson, *Summer for the Gods* (Cambridge, Mass.: Harvard University Press, 1997), 17.
[8] Ellen G. White, *Testimonies to the Church*, Vol. VIII, 256.
[9] Alister McGrath, *Christelijke Theologie* (Kampen: Uitgeverij Kok, 1998), 65.
[10] *Ibid.*, 225ff.
[11] *Seventh-day Adventist Hymnal*, hymn 198.
[12] Donald G. Bloesch, *The Almighty God: Power, Wisdom, Holiness, Love.* (Downer's Grove, Ill.: InterVarsity Press, 1995), 145-152.
[13] *Ibid.*, 154.
[14] Bloesch, 139, 140.
[15] Jon Dybdahl, *Old Testament Grace* (Nampa, Idaho: Pacific Press Publishing Association, 1990), 83.
[16] 'The Names of God in the Old Testament', in: *Seventh-day Adventist Bible Commentary*, vol. 1, 171.
[17] Jon Dybdahl, *Exodus* (Nampa, Idaho: Pacific Press Publishing Association, 1994), 55, 56.

Chapter Seven

# To Know God

Whether I like it or not, my name is included in dozens, possibly hundreds, of databases. Modern marketing relies to a large extent on being able to target specific groups. Someone who wants to target clergymen in Britain can buy a list that will, no doubt, contain my name and address. Credit bureaus know how I deal with my regular financial obligations. The fact that I read a particular newspaper is a welcome bit of information for those who are interested in my political sympathies. Amazon.com knows exactly what kind of books I like to buy. The British authorities know that I am a legal resident in their midst, who falls within a certain income-tax bracket, and my health insurer knows how my blood pressure fluctuates. My colleagues know at what time in the morning and afternoon I pause for a hot drink; my wife knows what food I like and dislike and that I hate shopping; and my children know I have great difficulty programming a VCR. Many people know my age and the fact that I drive a Fiat Marea, and that I have a slight problem controlling my waistline.

Some know just a few things about me, others a lot, but how many people really know me? How many really know what makes me tick? How I really feel about some aspects of my work? How many people know whether I am truly happy or just pretend to be? There is an immense difference between knowing about someone and knowing that person! We hardly know ourselves, our deepest drives and emotions, and at times we feel that we do not really know our nearest and dearest loved ones!

Likewise, we may know quite a few things about God on the basis of His general revelation and through the information provided by the Bible. But the question is: Do we really know Him or do we just know things *about* Him?

### God is a person

To suggest that we must know God rather than just having information about Him, implies the possibility of establishing a relationship with Him. And this, in turn, implies that God is a Some*one* rather than a Some*thing*. Traditional Christian teaching emphasizes that God is a person. But by now we have come to expect that human words, when applied to God, will need some further exploration.

The word "person" comes from the Latin word *persona*. Latin soon became the *lingua franca* of Christianity, comparable to the place the English language holds in the Adventist Church. But we must remember not only that the New Testament was originally written in Greek, but also that the earliest theologians of the church wrote their treatises and commentaries in Greek. The famous church father Tertullian (c. 160 - c. 220) was one of the first to write in Latin, and he invented the word *persona*. (He was apparently quite good at inventing new words; he is credited with having enriched the Latin language with 509 new nouns, 284 new adjectives, and 162 new verbs.[1]) Tertullian proposed the term *persona* to translate the Greek word *hypostasis*—a concept that was rather more vague than what we today would have in mind when describing a "person." *Hypostasis* would be more accurately rendered as "mode of manifestation." That helps to explain why in Roman times the Latin *persona* was later used to refer to theater masks, theater figures or roles. So, when the early church decided that God is a "person," this word did not quite mean what, on the surface, we would tend to assume. But it means certainly not less than what is expressed by our words "person" or "personality."

While dealing with the meaning of the word "person," we might as well look at two other terms. It is a basic Christian doctrine that God is a Trinity of three persons having one substance. We should be clear that the word "substance" (again from a Latin word—*substantia*) does not refer to anything material, but to "essence" or "being." The word "Trinity" is the English translation of yet another Latin word—*trinitas*—also coined by the second-century theologian Tertullian whom we have already met. *Trinitas* means a syndicate, a partnership of three, a trio. In today's language the doctrine of the Trinity tells us that the one and only true Christian God is in some mysterious way a oneness, but in a three-ness of different ways in which He relates to His creatures. It also tells us that this threeness never compromises the basic oneness of His divine being.

**Is the Trinity a biblical concept?**

How in the world can something as complicated as the doctrine of the Trinity help us understand who and what God is? Before we try to answer that question, we would do well to ask where we can find the roots of the doctrine of the Trinity. Do we find them in the Bible? For over a century the Jehovah's Witnesses have been shouting from the rooftops that there is no trace of this doctrine in the Scriptures. Among the more traditional churches, the Unitarians have also strongly denied the validity of the Trinity. Early Adventism was divided on the issue, but several prominent Adventist pioneers, for example James White and Uriah Smith, were decidedly anti-trinitarian in their theology! It took the Adventist Church until far into the nineteenth century to agree that the doctrine of the Trinity was indeed biblical and belonged among the fundamental Adventist beliefs.

Those who have done a little reading on the subject of the Trinity will know that one text in particular has often been quoted as proof for this doctrine—1 John 5:7, "There are three that bear record in heaven, the Father, the Word and the Holy Ghost; and these three are one" (KJV). This verse, however, has some real problems. Did you notice that I quoted it from the King James Version and not from the New International Version which I have used throughout this book? Do you know why I did so? Because the scholars who have translated the more recent Bible versions, such as the RSV and the NIV, have decided, on good grounds, that this statement is, in fact, a gloss. That is to say, these words were not part of the original manuscript, but were added later as a brief comment by a copyist, probably sometime in the second century. It is extremely interesting that at such an early date someone came to the conclusion expressed in this "gloss," but we must nonetheless be clear that this statement about the oneness of the three persons in the Godhead is not part of the authentic biblical text. That is the reason most recent Bible translators have dropped it from their Bible versions.

There are, however, a number of statements in the Bible that have become the building blocks for the doctrine of the Trinity.[2] The two most important texts are:

> "Therefore go and make disciples of all nations, baptizing them in the name of the *Father* and of the *Son* and of the *Holy Spirit*" (Matthew 28:19, emphasis added).
>
> May the grace of the Lord *Jesus Christ*, and the love of *God*, and the fellowship of the *Holy Spirit* be with you all (2 Corinthians 13:14, emphasis added).

Other texts also suggest that the doctrine of the Trinity is the all-pervasive pattern of divine action in the New Testament. There is a oneness in three-ness in "the totality of God's saving presence and power."[3] Look, for instance at the following passages:

> There are different kinds of gifts, but the same *Spirit*. There are different kinds of service, but the same *Lord*. There are different kinds of working, but the same *God* works all of them in all men (1 Corinthians 12:4-6, emphasis added).
>
> Consequently, you are no longer foreigners and aliens, but fellow citizens with *God*'s people and members of *God*'s household,

> built on the foundation of the apostles and prophets, with *Christ Jesus* himself as the chief cornerstone.
>
> In Him the whole building is joined together and rises to become a holy temple in the Lord.
>
> And in Him you too are being built together to become a dwelling in which God lives by his *Spirit* (Ephesians 2:19-22, emphasis added).

> But when the kindness and love of *God* our Savior appeared, He saved us, not because of righteous things we had done, but because of His mercy. He saved us through the washing of rebirth and renewal by the *Holy Spirit,* whom He poured out on us generously through *Jesus Christ* our Savior (Titus 3:4-6, emphasis added).

And there are yet other New Testament texts which mention this same threefold divine manifestation.[4] Many would also contend that there are even some traces of a Trinity doctrine in the Old Testament.[5]

Further evidence for a Trinity of three fully equal "persons" is found in the fact that the Bible often gives Jesus Christ, the Son, names and attributes that suggest He is fully God, on the same level as the Father—or, as the ancient church expressed it, that He is "very God of very God." And the Holy Spirit is also definitely more than merely an impersonal influence, as the theologians of the early church held and as many of the Adventist pioneers believed. In several instances, the Holy Spirit is described as on a par with the Father and the Son. He has attributes and participates in actions that make Him clearly a fully divine "person."

The Creation story contains an interesting allusion to the fact that more than one "person" was involved in the origin of life on this planet and of man in particular. Note the plural pronouns in the sentence: " 'Let *us* make man in our image, in our likeness' " (Genesis 1:26, emphasis added). In different places, the Bible attributes the creation of the world to the Father (Psalm 102:25), to the Son (Colossians 1:16; Hebrews 1:10), or to the Holy Spirit (Genesis 1:2; Psalm 104:30).[6]

The doctrine of the Trinity did not receive its traditional shape until the fourth and fifth centuries. Why did it take so long? The early church first wrestled with another, related, problem: Who and what was Jesus Christ? Was He human or divine? If He was both, as the early church eventually concluded on the basis of the biblical evidence, how did His human nature and His divine nature relate to each other? Was He, in fact, a split personality, or was He, in spite of His dual nature, truly one person? Other questions also arose: Had Christ existed together with the Father from all eternity? Or did He have a beginning? If He had no beginning, how could it then be said that He is God's Son? What does it mean when the Bible says that Christ is God's "only-begotten" Son? Should that phrase perhaps be explained as some sort of adoption of the human Christ into the Godhead?

A number of church councils convened to debate these and other questions, usually in response to some unorthodox claims regarding Christ's nature and person. Gradually, a generally accepted doctrine of Christ emerged. The creeds from the Council of Nicea (325) and the Council of Chalcedon (451) finally formulated the doctrine of Christ that was to be accepted by the vast majority of Christian churches.

After the church had dealt in a more or less final way with the questions that surrounded the person and nature of Christ, it was ready to study the topic of the Holy Spirit in more depth. The church finally agreed that the Spirit was also God in the fullest sense of the word, but it remained tragically divided over the question of whether the Spirit was related to the Son in the same way as the Spirit was related to the Father. It was partly over this very issue that in 1054 the eastern Church split from the western Church and that Christianity came to be divided into two major blocks.

Once the church had arrived at more or less satisfactory answers to the many questions surrounding Jesus Christ and the Holy Spirit, the next natural step was to further define the interrelationships between the Father, the Son, and the Holy Spirit. If all three are "persons," and fully divine, then how can Christians maintain that there is only one God? How can the aspect of "three-ness" and the aspect of "oneness" be reconciled? The doctrine of the Trinity was the eventual outcome of the church's study and debate on that matter.

We may find it somewhat difficult today to believe that generations, not only of theologians but also of common believers, could get excited about such theological minutiae. But Seventh-day Adventists should remember that our own church also had a hard time with these questions and took a long time to agree on these matters. Interestingly enough, it went through a similar process as did the early church—it eventually agreed that the classical statements about Christ were true, or at least provided the best formulations available; it then agreed with what had become the traditional doctrine of the Holy Spirit; and, finally, Adventists accepted the doctrine of the Trinity. Though apparently still reluctant to actually use the term "Trinity," Ellen G. White expressed in 1905 what by then had become accepted Adventist teaching: "There are three living persons in the heavenly Trio . . . the Father, the Son and the Holy Spirit."[7]

**Do we need this doctrine?**

If the doctrine of the Trinity is not explicitly taught in the Bible, and if it is apparently so difficult and complicated that it took the early church a number of centuries to formulate it and later took Adventism considerable time to accept it, why have it? The answer is that once you have looked at all the alternatives, the doctrine of the Trinity is unavoidable.

Christians, who believe in the Bible, must never lose sight of the fundamental fact that there is only one God. This basic insight of Judaism—"The Lord our God, the Lord is one" (Deuteronomy 6:4)—was carried over into the Christian faith. But Christian believers also had to account for a divine Christ and a divine Holy Spirit. How did these two relate to God the Father? Various wrong answers developed; these usually went in either of two directions. Either they did not respect the fundamental oneness of God, or, in order to protect that fundamental oneness, they compromised the three-ness of the Godhead.

# OUR AWESOME GOD

Some heresies in the early church tried to safeguard God's oneness by suggesting that the one divine Being could assume, at different times, three different roles. Technically, this idea that God can wear three different masks—that of Father, Son, and Spirit—is called *modalism*. This concept is attractive because it stresses the truth of God's oneness. But, fortunately, the early church realized that this approach could not be regarded as a full expression of God's revelation to us. The distinctiveness of the saving work of the Savior and of the Holy Spirit must be maintained and may not be sacrificed.

Others, in defending the three-ness of the Godhead, ended up by believing in virtually three gods. Thus they became stranded in a Christian form of polytheism (technically referred to as *tri-theism*—the belief in three gods).

The doctrine of the Trinity steers a middle course. It refuses to emphasize the oneness at the expense of the three-ness, but it also refuses to acknowledge the three-ness at the expense of the oneness.

The doctrine of the Trinity is one of the great paradoxes of the Christian faith, but it is not the only one. The dictionary describes a paradox as "an assertion that is essentially self-contradictory, though based on a valid deduction from acceptable premises," or as "a seemingly contradictory statement that may nonetheless be true."

Most of us have something against paradoxes. It goes against the grain of our modern logic. But a purely rational approach will get us nowhere when we are dealing with such concepts as the Trinity. It has been rightly said that "whatever you can grasp in your mind you can be sure that it is not God!"[8] And the same writer went on to point out that "the deeper we enter into the infinite, the better we understand that we can never hold it in our hands."[9] With our finite human understanding we must realize that at times we cannot reconcile certain seemingly contradictory statements.

I believe that Christ is fully divine and became fully human. It seems to my limited intelligence that the one would exclude the other, yet in faith I confess that somehow both statements are true. The same applies to the written Word, the Bible. It is a product of divine inspiration, yet, at the same time, it is the collective work of some forty human authors. It would seem impossible to combine these two elements logically, yet in faith I know that somehow both assertions are true. Likewise, in faith I accept the paradox of the Trinity: God is one. He is one in three "persons," yet, He is one.

It may well be that modern Christians—Adventists most definitely included—should be more balanced in their approach to the mystery of God. I suspect that many of us need to learn to use not only the left half of our brains that wants to analyze and define, but also to develop the right hemisphere of our brains that steers our intuition and helps us to know in non-rational ways. The prophet in us needs the assistance of the poet![10] Those who do not shy away from a difficult book, should spend some time with Rudolf Otto's classical study *The Idea of the Holy*.[11] It is a powerful reminder that God should always be approached with a sense of awe and deep reverence, even with a sense of religious rapture and exaltation. After all, He is an awesome God.

That does not mean that we should tremble before Him with fear or that we should not probe with our minds what His Word has revealed. But it does mean that when all is said and done, there should be a deep sense of mystery when we step into the presence of the One who is utterly holy.

### The Father-Son-Holy Spirit God

Father, Son and Holy Spirit—somehow They are separate, yet inseparable. Somehow They are three, and yet They are one. Let me repeat it once more: in our contemplation of this mystery, we must remember that we know about God only what He has decided to reveal to us. And the truth is that God has, over time, revealed Himself to us as Father, as Son, and as Holy Spirit. Evidently, He wanted us to realize that He is the one almighty God who is in heaven. The God, who lives in a realm of His own. The God who is not to be equated with all that exists, but who Himself created, supports, and pervades everything that is. We must also realize that when He entered our world as our Savior, heaven did not become empty. In spite of His unfathomable act of self-emptying in the Incarnation, He remained the God of heaven and earth. And, once the plan of salvation entered into a new phase, after the Resurrection and the Ascension, the everlasting divine presence of God among mankind could be experienced more directly and intensely. It is in His relationship to us on planet Earth that He is the Father-Son-Holy Spirit God. We do not know whether He has revealed Himself in the same way to other parts of the universe, but that is how He has revealed Himself to us.

The fourth-century church father Gregory of Nazianzus said, "When I say 'God,' I mean Father, Son, and Holy Spirit."[12] In fact, one modern theologian, Robert Jensen, has proposed that we should regard "Father-Son-Holy Spirit" as the proper name of the Christian God.[13]

### The Father

Throughout the Bible, God is called "Father." Even in Old Testament times God was referred to as "Father." Moses asked his people the question: Is God not "your Father, your Creator, who made you and formed you?" (Deuteronomy 32:6). And Isaiah exclaimed, "But You are our Father . . . You, O Lord, are our Father, our Redeemer from of old is Your name" (63:16). In the New Testament, God is constantly referred to as "Father," as the Father of Jesus Christ. In the Gospels Christ refers about 170 times to His Father and gives us the good news that He is the One to whom we human beings may also pray: " 'Our Father in heaven, hallowed be your name' " (Matthew 6:9).

Today, many object to depicting God as "Father;" they feel this metaphor belongs to a time when men called all the shots and women were of little value. Calling God, "Father," they say, is to re-enforce the patriarchal value system which discriminated against women. It also does grave injustice to God, they argue, who should not be thought of in male terms. John Shelby Spong, the radical Episcopalian bishop of Newark, New Jersey, says that the use of the word "Father" to refer to God offends him deeply. "I do not care to worship a God defined by masculinity," he says.[14] Radical feminist theologian Mary Daly seems to be quoted wherever and whenever this issue is discussed: "If God is male, then male is God. The divine patriarch castrates women as long as He is allowed to live on in the human imagination."[15]

Feminist theologians often argue that the patriarchal God of the Bible is powerful, dominant, and implacable. There may be some truth in the claim that the picture of God as Father can easily lead to a distorted concept of Him, in particular in societies where men are totally in charge and fathers are to be blindly obeyed. And the insistence of feminist theologians that we must also look at the more feminine aspects of God's character is a fair comment. Humanity was created in God's image as both male and female, and thus there is every reason to point out that somehow the uniqueness of both genders reflects something of the divine nature. We do well to remember the texts, though they are few, that speak about God in feminine terms. In His anxiety for His people, God compares Himself to "a woman in childbirth," who cries out, gasps and pants (Isaiah 42:14) and to a mother who cannot "forget the baby at her breast" (Isaiah 49:15). And He makes the telling statement: " 'As a mother comforts her child, so will I comfort you; and you will be comforted over Jerusalem' " (Isaiah 66:13).

But note that although God is *compared* with a mother, He is never *addressed* as Mother in either the Old or New Testaments! Speaking about God as Mother carries the real danger of identifying the creation with the Creator ("Mother Earth"). This is, indeed, exactly what has happened with many radical feminists "who have abandoned the Christian church and faith altogether, and [have] a view of divinity that is [more] at home in modern witches' covens" than in Christianity.[16]

The fact that God is referred to as Father has nothing to do with gender. The God of the Bible has no sexuality. Protesting against such male terms as "Father" and substituting female language for them would suggest that God does have sexuality.[17] Numbers 23:19 states: " 'God is not a man . . . nor the son of a man,' " and Deuteronomy 4:15, 16 warns us not to picture God as either male or female.

The metaphor of God's fatherhood is a beautiful pointer to His care and protection; it would be a terrible pity to lose sight of this.

**The Son**

The opening paragraph of the letter to the Hebrews says it all:

> In the past God spoke to our forefathers through the prophets at many times and in various ways, but in these last days He has spoken to us by His Son, whom He appointed heir of all things, and through whom He made the universe. The Son is the radiance of God's glory and the exact representation of his being (1:1-3).

God reveals Himself to some extent in nature. He revealed Himself more fully through His spokespersons in Old Testament times, but Jesus is the ultimate revelation of what God is like. Jesus Christ, the man who gave His name to Christianity, was not a human being like us, but was and is our incarnate God. Jesus Himself said, "Anyone who has seen me, has seen the Father" (John 14:9). So if you want to know what God is like, look at Jesus, read His life story and meditate upon it, study His character, and then say to yourself. "Yes, that is what God is like. That is how He cares for us and how He loves us!"

> Christ came to the world to reveal the character of God, to make plain to us His paternal love toward His adopted children. We are not to estimate the character of God by the stupendous works of nature alone, but by the simple, lovely life of Jesus, who presented Jehovah as more merciful, more compassionate, more tender, than our earthly parents. Jesus presented the Father as one to whom we could give our confidence and present our wants. When we are in terror of God and overwhelmed with the thought of His glory and majesty, the Father points us to Christ as His representative. What you see revealed in Jesus of tenderness, compassion, and love, is the reflection of the attributes of the

Father. The cross of Calvary reveals to man the love of God. Christ represents the Sovereign of the universe as a God of love.[18]

**The Holy Spirit**

God created the universe and everything that is; He continues to uphold it. He became one with us when a remedy was needed to help us escape from the terrible predicament of sin. He is the One who sticks with us, constantly and in a very direct way. He helps us to distinguish right from wrong. He urges us to seek Him. When we cannot find the right words to speak to Him, He comes to our aid. He inspires us when we are asked to give account of our faith. He provides us with the skills that we need to fulfill our roles in the faith community to which we belong.

The Holy Spirit-God, who was ever present with mankind, is even closer to all men and women of good will since the days of Christ than before. And we have the promise that in the final stages of Earth's history, before the world comes to its end, that presence will intensify in new and surprising ways.

We have not been able to solve the mystery of the Trinity. But in faith we can accept its glorious truth—God is One. There is no other God beside Him. He comes to us in His magnificent three-ness of being—Father, Son, and Holy Spirit. This three-in-one God is all we need.

---

[1] Alister McGrath, *Christelijke Theologie* (Kampen: Uitgeverij Kok, 1997), 265.

[2] *Ibid.*, 262-284.

[3] *Ibid.*, 265.

[4] See e.g. 2 Cor. 1:21-22; Gal. 4:6; 2 Thess. 2 :13,14. 1 Pet. 1:2.

[5] God is referred to as personified in three different ways: as 'Wisdom' (see e.g. Proverbs 1:20-23; 3:19: 9:1-6; Job 28); as the Word of God (see e.g. Ps. 119:89; 147:15-20; Isa. 55:1-11); and as the Spirit of God (see e.g. Isa. 42:1-3; Ps. 104:30; Ez. 36:27; 37:1-14).

[6] Father, Son and Holy Spirit are all referred to as 'God'; see Matt. 11:25-27; John 6:27; Rom. 1:7; John 1:1, 14; Tit. 2:13; Heb. 1:8; Acts 5:3-9. All three are depicted as omniscient (Rom. 11:33; Rev. 2:23; 1 Cor. 2:11), and each is presented as being equal to the others (Matt. 28:19; John 10:30; 2 Cor. 13:14; Eph. 4:4-6).

[7] Ellen G. White, *Evangelism*, 615.

[8] Henri de Lubac, *The Discovery of God* (Edinburgh: T&T Clark, 1996 ed.), 111.

[9] *Ibid.*, 117.
[10] *Ibid.*, 98.
[11] Rudolf Otto, *The Idea of the Holy* (New York: Oxford University Press, 1958 ed.).
[12] Donald G. Bloesch, *God the Almighty* (Downers Grove, Ill.: InterVarsity Press, 1995), 166.
[13] See McGrath, 279.
[14] John Shelby Spong, *Why Christianity Must Change or Die* (New York: HarperCollins Publishers, 1998), 5.
[15] Mary Daly, *Beyond God the Father: Toward a Philosophy of Women's Liberation* (Boston, Mass.: Beacon Press, 1973), 19.
[16] Elizabeth Achtemeier, 'Exchanging God for "No Gods": A Discussion of Female Language for God', in: Alvin F. Kimel, ed., *Speaking the Christian God—The Holy Trinity and the Challenge of Feminism* (Grand Rapids, Mich.: William B. Eerdmans Publishing Company, 1992), 13.
[17] *Ibid.*, 4.
[18] Ellen G. White, *Youth Instructor*, 22 September, 1892.

**Chapter Eight**

# People Who Believe

The assurance that God is a person is a tremendous encouragement. It means a relationship may be within our reach. That brings us to our next question: Can we hope to establish this relationship, and, if so, how? What do we do to make contact with this one and only triune God whom we have tried to describe in the previous three chapters? Is there something we ourselves can do to establish a relationship with God? Again we meet a paradox, for the answer is *Yes* and *No*.

*No*, because in any relationship between man and God, God is always the One who takes the initiative. Before we can ever hope to find Him, He has already found us. God already loves us before we love Him. He says, " 'I have loved you with an everlasting love' " (Jeremiah 31:3). Isaiah makes the same point (Isaiah 65:1) in words directed to Israel. "To a nation that did not call on my name, I said, 'Here am I, here am I.' " But since Paul quotes Isaiah's words in his letter to the Roman Christians (10:20), we may confidently apply the message also to ourselves: "I revealed myself to those who did not ask for me; I was found by those who did not seek me."

In a somewhat unusual, but striking manner, Pheme Perkins, a professor of theology at Boston College, expresses God's persistence in getting us to accept His love. He says, "Finding God is not the problem . . . God is more like the nasty black fly behind my ear when jogging. The question is rather 'How to get rid of God?' "[1]

So, one answer to our question—Is there something we ourselves can do to establish a relationship with God?—is *No*. God has already taken the initiative to establish a relationship with us.

But the answer to that questions is also *Yes*, because God wants to be sought! Because we have a free will, we can decide to move toward Him or to run away from Him. God's search for us may well remain hidden if we do not make the decision to search for Him—a search that will be successful. Listen again to one of God's spokespersons addressing people who had been turning their backs on God for a long time: " 'You will call upon me and come and pray to me, and I will listen to you. You will seek me . . . and find me when you seek me with all your heart' " (Jeremiah 29:12-13). Listen, also, to the promise of Christ Himself: " 'Ask and it will be given to you; seek and you will find; knock and the door will be opened to you' " (Matthew 7:7).

**Finding God**

Men and women have fallen in love in the strangest places. But most would agree that romance has a better chance at a candle-lit dinner than during a chance meeting in a supermarket. It is possible to study while standing in line at the post office, but a quiet spot in the library provides an atmosphere that is much more conducive to academic endeavors. Likewise, if we seek for a spot to meditate and concentrate our minds on higher things, we do better during evensong in a cathedral than in the New York subway.

In the fascinating book *Finding God*,[2] James Martin has brought together some seventy short (some ultra-short) essays from all sorts of men and women, who give their own personal answers to the question of how people can best find God. Although people search for God along diverse routes and find Him in different ways, a number of aspects are mentioned over and over again by those who—in the famous words of

C. S. Lewis—have been "surprised by joy"[3] as they encountered their God.

When the Old Testament prophet Elijah had a special encounter with the Almighty, he found that God was not in the thunder or in the earthquake, but in "a gentle whisper" (1 Kings 19:12). Similarly, many have found that silence, rather than overpowering, or even supernatural, phenomena, has been the prelude to an experience with God. " 'Be still,' " God says, " 'and know that I am God' " (Psalm 46:10).

Reading the Bible is always an important link in the process of finding God. At first sight, it would appear unlikely that people who know little or nothing about God or religion would be able to read such a seemingly difficult book with profit. But something happens when people go to the Word with the hope and expectation of getting to know God. In some mysterious way, the same Spirit who inspired the authors who acted as God's "penmen,"[4] also enlightens the hearts and minds of those who read these words with an openness to the Beyond. It is not primarily our painstaking efforts to understand, but the fact that God graciously comes to us through His Word, that makes the reading of the Bible such an important element in our search for Him.

Putting ourselves in an environment where God is worshiped in song and prayer has also proven to be an important element in finding God. Regular church attendance has brought many to a close encounter with the Lord of the universe. Rabbi Michael Lerner, a well-known New York Jewish author, adds a dimension with which many Adventists will wholeheartedly agree, but which some of us have yet to experience fully:

> Take off every Sabbath and spend that entire day celebrating and standing in awe of the grandeur of the universe. Have nothing to do with any other goals on that day. Don't deal with money, or "power over." Instead, only respond with joy and with amazement. Open yourself to that which is beyond categories and that which cannot be fully expressed in language. Go inward, but also go

> outward. Expand your consciousness. Make this day a day of communal celebration, but also take many hours totally by yourself for inward meditation or outward joy.[5]

We also encounter God through our commitment to other people, in particular to those in dire need. The same rabbi we just quoted, states as his strong belief that we "find God by becoming a partner with God."[6]

Sister Helen Prejean, since 1982 a spiritual adviser of inmates on death row, gives us the same message: "The most direct road that I have found to God is in the faces of poor and struggling people." And Jim Wallis of *Sojourners* magazine underlines this truth with similar words: "We must accept physical contact with the poor as one of the spiritual disciplines, like reading the Bible and prayer."[7]

Martin E. Marty, professor at the University of Chicago, who has written extensively on the place of religion in American society, is right when he argues that we should not approach our search for God with a sense of despair, almost expecting to fail. I like the way he suggests God can be found as we are enjoying the life He gave us:

> How does God find me? If God is, but is ineffable, beyond beyondness, self-contained, forget it. Then God is unfindable. Rather than seek God, eat pomegranates, shoot pool, listen to Scarlatti, munch almonds, watch fireflies, visit the Andes. If God is, and is ineffable, beyond the gods but still relational, remember it. Then God is findable. While seeking God, eat pomegranates, etc.[8]

**Join the crowd**

A popular chapter in the New Testament is Hebrews 11 which presents us with a gallery of heroes of faith. It starts with men such as Abel, Enoch, and Noah, and includes a long list of other men and women of Old Testament times who kept the faith, often despite considerable odds. It is against this background that the writer follows with the exhortation at the beginning of the next chapter: "Therefore, since we are surrounded by such a great cloud of witnesses," let us remain faithful and "let us run with perseverance the race marked out for us. Let us fix our eyes on Jesus, the author and perfecter of our faith" (Hebrews 12:1, 2).

Believers have often felt like the prophet Elijah after his climactic experience on Mount Carmel, when he had to face the terrifying reality of the hatred of Queen Jezebel. He felt great pity for himself, fearing that he was the only true believer God had left on this planet. But God corrected that false impression. Yes, Elijah was part of a minority, but the group was not as small as he thought. There were still another 7,000 men and women who had not compromised their belief in the one and true God (1 Kings 19:18).

Today many Christians, particularly in the Western world, feel rather despondent. Belief in the Christian God does not seem to be part of the postmodern agenda at the beginning of a new millennium. But, though faith is often a scarce commodity, there are—praise God!—still thousands, or even millions, who together form an enormous "cloud of witnesses." Many of these will remain anonymous—simple men and women who live their faith according to the light they have received, faithful to their conscience and to what they understand as the divine will for their lives. But our time also has numerous high profile personalities—men and women who have excelled in the arts, in science, in business, or even in politics—who have found God early or late in life and who proudly acknowledge their relationship with Him. Space will permit me to mention only a few of them.

### Susan Howatch

Shortly after I moved to Great Britain, I discovered *Glittering Images,* the first book of an impressive series of six novels, full of drama and suspense, but also of religion and church politics, set against the background of the more conservative wing of the Anglican Church. Living in the close of the cathedral in Salisbury, Britain, author Susan Howatch is herself almost part of the milieu she portrays so skillfully.

Only more recently did I become aware of the fact that Susan Howatch is a committed Christian.[9]

Though Susan Howatch studied law, her ambition was to become a writer. After years of rejection slips, she finally had a manuscript accepted. That first novel became a huge success. But financial prosperity did not bring happiness. Seeing her marriage break down and feeling increasingly perplexed, she began her search for God in earnest, and while she "was being stripped down . . . God was closing in." She wanted to know more about God, and began to read everything about Christianity and theology she could lay her hands on. She even took a formal university course to figure out what God wanted her to do with her life. She went through what she describes as "a classical conversion" experience and joined the Church of England. Subsequently, she has endowed a lectureship in theology at the University of Cambridge with £1 million ($1.6 million). She sets time aside for daily private meditation and attends church every day.

Some of the theological ideas Susan Howatch espouses may not be totally biblical, but there seems to be no doubt that she has encountered the incomparable, unique, triune God and has embarked on a life-long journey with Him.

### Delia Smith

Another writer I had never thought of as a Christian is Delia Smith, the famous British cookery writer with over ten million copies of her books in print, and the presenter of gourmet cooking programs on television for more than twenty-five years. Her weekly BBC program is highly popular, and her books on sophisticated home cooking are also selling well in the United States. But, remarkably enough, among her best-selling books is a rather different work that has been described as "a spiritual classic for today." It is a book about prayer, titled *A Journey Into God.*[10] Reading this book, one cannot remain in any doubt that Delia Smith knows God. Not the life-stifler God, nor the God of fear and anxiety, nor the cuddly-bear God, nor the God of the fit and the strong, but the God who is the divine Word, our Friend and Lover, with whom we can have a life-long relationship.

# People Who Believe

**Alvin Plantinga**

Alvin Plantinga is one of today's most prominent philosophers of religion.[11] He has taught at such prestigious academic institutions as Yale and Harvard, but has also worked for some twenty years at Calvin College, the intellectual center of the Reformed branch of Christianity in the United States. Presently, he holds the John A. O'Brien Chair of Philosophy and is the director of the Center for Philosophy of Religion at the University of Notre Dame, near South Bend, Indiana.

Born in 1932 in Ann Arbor, Michigan, Alvin Plantinga grew up and was educated in a strict Dutch Reformed milieu. It was not until he began his graduate studies at Harvard that he encountered serious non-Christian thought and began to entertain acute doubts about God's existence. But not for long! One gloomy January evening he walked across the campus to his residency hall, and his doubts were dissolved in a drastic manner:

> It was dark, windy, raining, nasty. But suddenly it was as if the heavens opened; I heard, so it seemed, music of overwhelming power and grandeur and sweetness; there was light of unimaginable splendor and beauty; it seemed I could see into heaven itself; and I suddenly saw or perhaps felt with great clarity and persuasion and conviction that the Lord was really there and was all I had thought. The effects of this experience lingered for a long time: I was still caught up in arguments about the existence of God, but they often seemed to me merely academic, of little existential concern.[12]

Today, many years of teaching and several highly complicated books later, Plantinga is still a believer. Like most of us, he wrestles from time to time with questions for which he has no answers. What has he found most profitable in his search for God? "I wish I could report something more exciting," he says, "but I find Sunday School a genuine occasion for learning and spiritual growth."[13]

### Glenn Loury

If I had to list the ten books that have meant the most to me over the last five years, *The Search for God at Harvard*, by *New York Times'* religion reporter Ari L. Goldmann would most definitely be on that list.[14] The book is beautifully written and offers a surprising and extraordinary insight into the diversity of religious explorations and the "variety of religious experience" in what was at one time a bastion of traditional Christian piety. But beyond this, Goldmann's struggle to live according to his own orthodox Jewish principles in a world that, more often than not, did not understand why he would be so strict on certain religious issues, provides an extremely fascinating parallel strand that runs through this book. It somehow closely resembles the kind of experience many a Seventh-day Adventist has had as he tries to live his faith in his professional environment.

A few years after Goldmann wrote his book, Kelly Monroe, a chaplain for graduate students at Harvard, decided there was more to the search for God at this famous university than one would conclude from Goldmann's book. So she decided to add another dimension to his picture. Her book, *Finding God at Harvard*, chronicles the spiritual journeys of forty-two faculty members, students, and former students. It wants to explode the myth that Christian faith cannot survive a rigorous intellectual atmosphere. Monroe's book misses the literary beauty and the unique fascination of Goldmann's book, but it does contain remarkable and inspiring stories about men and women who either have found the Christian God or who have kept their faith in Him while pursuing an academic career in a largely secular context. One of the stories that especially impressed me was that of Glenn Loury, who previously taught economics at Harvard's Kennedy School of Government and who is presently professor of economics at Boston University.[15]

Loury recounts his professional success—in the eyes of his colleagues, being a tenured professor at Harvard was the pinnacle of his profession. He had research grants and enjoyed great prestige. But there was no real joy. "My achievements gave me no sense of fulfillment.

Nothing in my life had any sense of depth and meaning." He had problems with drugs and alcohol, to the point where they began to threaten his health and his reputation. His marriage was in trouble.

But then things began to change. Loury puts it in very simple words: "What happened to me was that some people came forward to offer me words about the gospel of Jesus Christ." While he was a patient in a substance abuse program in a psychiatric hospital, a young nurse gently helped him to rediscover the faith of his childhood and brought him back into the church.

> There was no one particular moment when the skies opened up and God came wafting down. Rather, over the months as I began to study the Bible, as I went to church, as I learned to pray, as I began to reflect honestly on my life, and as I began to open myself up to the Spirit of God to minister to me and to move me, I came to realize that there was something dramatic missing in my life.[16]

Glenn Loury was converted. His life changed. Relationships were healed. His marriage not only survived, but came to life. In addition, Loury found genuine satisfaction in his academic work. "This knowledge of God's unconditional love for humankind provides the moral grounding for my work in cultural and racial reconciliation, economics and justice."[17]

### Malcolm Muggeridge

Born in 1903, Malcolm Muggeridge grew up and was educated in Cambridge, Britain. He started his career as a university lecturer in India and Egypt, but earned his fame as a journalist for a number of British newspapers. Having been raised in a strongly socialist environment, he became infatuated with communism. But witnessing the terrible Ukranian famine in the winter of 1932, while he was a correspondent in Moscow, ended his admiration for the communist ideology.

Muggeridge died in 1990, but his books are still widely read, in particular his *Something Beautiful for God*, a lovely literary portrait of Mother Teresa, and his *Jesus Rediscovered*, in which he describes his spiritual journey from being a total skeptic to becoming one of the twentieth century's leading apologists for the Christian faith. His conversion to Christianity took place in the 1960s.

> It was while I was in the Holy Land for the purpose of making three BBC programmes on the New Testament that a curious, almost magical certainty seized me about Jesus' birth, ministry and crucifixion . . . I became aware that there really had been a man, Jesus, who was also God—I was conscious of His presence. He really had spoken those sublime words—I heard them.[18]

People around Muggeridge failed to understand what had happened to him. Old friends would shake their heads and speak to him "with kindly compassion, as they would if I had been run in for indecent exposure in Hyde Park," but Muggeridge never turned back from the road of faith. His life-long search to better understand the Christian God had begun. In a sublime 1966 article in the *New Statesmen*, he testified of that new-found faith. "God," he said, came "padding after me like a Hound of heaven." There was no escape.

Muggeridge referred to himself as "a theological ignoramus." Well, he may not have known much *about* God (although he clearly was too modest when making this claim), but he very evidently knew God. He knew Him as

> . . . a being with whom one has a relationship, on the one hand, inconceivably more personal than the most intimate human one, to the point that, as we are told, God has actually counted the hairs of each head; on the other hand, so remote that in order to establish a valid relationship at all, it is necessary to die . . . to batter down one's ego as one might a deadly snake . . .
>
> What can be said with certainty is that, once the confrontation has been experienced—the rocky summit climbed, the

interminable desert crossed—an unimaginable delectable vista presents itself, so vast, so luminous, so enchanting, that the small ecstasies of human love, and the small satisfactions of human achievement, by comparison pale into insignificance.[19]

**Jimmy Carter**

Having lived twice for some time in the United States, I have developed an intense interest in American politics. Unlike most Americans, I have come to the conclusion that Jimmy Carter was probably one of the best American presidents of the twentieth century. (Please continue to read even if you disagree!) Unfortunately—from my perspective—the terrible mishap that took place during the effort to rescue the hostages in the Teheran embassy prevented him from getting a second term in office.

Whether or not one agrees with my rather high opinion of Carter as a political leader, most Americans would be willing to concede that he was probably the most morally principled president of America in the post-World War II period. I had heard about Carter's faith and his role as a Sunday School teacher in his local church, but had not been aware of the depth of his religious conviction until I picked up his latest book, *Living Faith*[20]—his eleventh, but most personal book yet.

In this simple, but genuine book, the former U.S. president tells about his early years—how he grew up with Christian values and accepted Jesus Christ at age eleven during a revival service and was baptized the following Sunday; how his religious experience matured; and how he became an active church member. He recounts how he met Rosalyn, began a promising career in the navy, but returned to his native Plains after his father's death to start a farm warehouse for peanut farmers. And he describes how he decided to run for public office, first at the local and state levels, and later at the national level.

Standing up for his principles—in particular for his belief in equal rights for people of different ethnic backgrounds—at times cost him dearly. And later in the Oval Office, decision making was often a lonely and heart-rending experience. But Jimmy Carter had his special resource:

> I have had to confront physical danger, financial despair, family tragedy, political failure, and quandaries concerning my career. In all such crises, self-analysis, self-questioning, and prayer have been the heart of my approach.[21]

What probably impressed me most in the book was the section about the ex-president's peace-making efforts through the Carter Center and his untiring support for the Habitat for Humanity program that has resulted in more than 50,000 homes for as many needy families. But even more impressive were his less-known but touching experiences during two mission assignments, when he went from door to door, visiting hundreds of homes to tell people about faith in God and salvation in Christ.

President Carter expresses his faith in less sophisticated ways than writers such as Malcolm Muggeridge. But his testimony is just as impressive:

> Except during my childhood, when I was probably influenced by Michelangelo's Sistine Chapel depiction of God with a flowing white beard, I have never tried to project the Creator in any kind of human likeness. The vociferous debates about whether God is male or female seem ridiculous to me. I think of God as an omnipotent and omniscient presence, a spirit that permeates the universe, the essence of truth, nature, being, and life. To me, these are profound and indescribable concepts that seem to be trivialized when expressed in words.
>
> At the same time, I feel a need for a personal relationship and an ability to communicate with God. As a Christian, I have additional knowledge about God from New Testament Scripture: "God is love" (1 John 4:8) and what Jesus told his questioning disciples: "If you have seen me, you have seen the Father" (John 14:9).

**Millions of others**

These are just a few examples of high-profile believers that have emerged from some of my recent reading. It would not be difficult to point to many others in all walks of life who have found the one and only true God and who have made Him the center of their existence. They number in the millions and live all over the world. In spite of rampant materialism and secularism, many men and women today have searched for God and have been found by Him. The author of Hebrews 12:1 was right; there is indeed a "cloud of witnesses". If you have not already done so, make sure to join the crowd!

---

[1] James Martin, *Finding God* (Ligouri, Miss: Triumph Books, 1997), 14.
[2] 2. See note 1.
[3] He gave this title to one of his best-known books.
[4] A term used by Ellen G. White. See e.g.: *Selected Messages*, vol. 1, 21.
[5] Martin, 12.
[6] *Ibid.*, 10.
[7] *Ibid.*, 1,3.
[8] Martin, 151.
[9] Through reading Anne Bancroft's book *Women in Search of the Sacred* (London: Penguin Books, 1996), 38-56.
[10] (London: Hodder & Stoughton, 1988).
[11] Alvin Plantinga, 'A Christian Life Partly Lived', in: Kelly James Clark, ed., *Philosophers who Believe* (Downers Grove, Ill.: InterVarsity Press, 1993), 45-82.
[12] *Ibid.*, 51,52.
[13] *Ibid.*, 67.
[14] ( New York: Ballantine Books, 1991).
[15] Kelly Monroe, ed., *Finding God at Harvard* (Grand Rapids, Mich: Zondervan Publishing House, 1996), 67-76.
[16] *Ibid.*, 73.
[17] *Ibid.*, 76.
[18] Malcolm Muggeridge, *Jesus Rediscovered* (Glasgow: Fount Paperbacks, 1985 ed.), 1.
[19] *Ibid.*, 43,44.
[20] (New York: Times Books, 1996).
[21] *Ibid.*, 104.

## Chapter Nine

# If God Is Love, Why . . . ?

Serving as the rabbi for the Jewish community in Natick, Massachusetts, Harold S. Kushner knew about illness and death. He did what he could to help the six hundred families in his pastoral care to cope with their loss and grief. But nothing had prepared him and his wife for the shock that came when they were told their three-year-old son would not live beyond age twelve—or age fifteen at the most. Little Aaron was suffering from a rare, but fatal, disease: progeria. He would never grow taller than about one meter, would not get any hair on his head or elsewhere on his body, and would look about ten times his actual age. After Aaron died at age fourteen, Rabbi Kushner wrote a book, *When Bad Things Happen to Good People*, in which he wrestled with that vexing, age-old question: How can we explain the bad things that happen to good people?

Kushner and his wife are not unique. Many of us have had more than a fair share of suffering and misfortune. I suppose that according to the law of averages, I have had my portion of tragedy. As a ten-year-old boy, I lost my brother who was two years younger. When I was fourteen, my father died after a long and ugly fight with leukemia. Later, a brother-in-law was hit and killed by a reckless driver, and my youngest sister died at age 32 from a brain tumor, leaving a husband and three young children behind. I realize, however, that many others have experienced far more misery in their lives than I have. For some, life is simply one long succession of disease, despair, and death.

**The problem of suffering**

The question of why so much misery exists not only finds expression in the heart-rending cries of those directly affected, but has also posed a tremendous intellectual challenge to philosophers and theologians. If God knows everything and if He is so powerful that nothing is impossible for Him, why does He allow all those devastating earthquakes and deadly hurricanes? Why does He allow people to suffer from cancer, heart attacks, and Alzheimer's disease? Why do people get killed in car crashes or in work-related accidents? Why do people hate and murder? Why Hiroshima? Why Auschwitz? Why Northern Ireland? Why the genocide in Rwanda and the Balkans? Why mass shootings in schools or offices?

The problem of suffering is not a new dilemma that has suddenly emerged in modern times. Lactantius, a Christian philosopher in the third century, provided the classical expression of the dilemma, using terms which, in fact, go back to the Latin orator Cicero:

> If God wants to suppress evil and cannot do so, it is because He is not omnipotent, and that is a contradiction. If He can do so and does not will to, it is because He does not love us, and that is equally a contradiction. If He cannot and does not will to do so, it is that He has neither power nor love and therefore is not God. And if He can do so and wills to do so, how is it that there is evil and why does He not suppress it?[1]

A contemporary French philosopher, Paul Ricoeur, repeats the same question in his book on evil:

> How can one affirm together, without contradiction, the following three propositions: God is all-powerful; God is absolutely good; yet

> evil exists . . . when only two of these propositions are compatible, never all three?[2]

The "why" question has been asked millions of times and in a multitude of different ways—by crying mothers as well as by learned scholars. As the centuries have gone by, the questioning has tended to become more defiant, and a growing resistance has developed against a sadistic God who claims to have all power and pretends to be all love, and yet apparently turns a blind eye to the terrible suffering on planet Earth.

Of course, various solutions have been suggested. Theologians and philosophers have developed theodicies. (The dictionary defines the term "theodicy" as "the branch of theology concerned with defending the attributes of God against objections resulting from physical and moral evil.") Gottfried Wilhelm Leibnitz (1646-1716), the German philosopher, mathematician, and statesman who still is regarded as one of the supreme intellects of the seventeenth century, was the first thinker to actually use the word *theodicy*. Ever since, it has been the technical term to refer to ongoing attempts to find an intellectually defensible formula which recognizes the reality of evil and suffering without compromising either the power or the love of God.

In an earlier chapter, we encountered one modern theological school—process theology—that has tried to come to terms with the dilemma. Process theologians have argued that God is powerful and knows a lot, but that He is not *all*-powerful and does not know everything. This position, they claim, is the only viable option if one wants to maintain faith in God in the face of all the evil in the world. But a God who learns as He goes along is not the one and only true Christian God that is worthy of our prayers and adoration.

For some, the answer is still found in the traditional Calvinistic doctrine of divine providence. Things happen because God has decreed all events from eternity. There is nothing we can do about it. God looks after those He has elected for eternal salvation and destroys those who are not among His elect. Those who are damned have nothing to complain about; they get what they deserve. And those who are saved have nothing to brag about; they get what God in His grace decides to give them.

Just recently I read on an Internet site a layman's version of this way of thinking. Here is how someone, who goes by the name Orin L. Moses III, explains why tragedies happen, taking a plane crash as his example. The collective destinies of all people on board brought them together for this tragic event. It is one of these unfortunate things that cannot be avoided in an imperfect world. Most passengers perish. They do not qualify for salvation because they have persisted in their unbelief, therefore they were expendable according to God's foreknowledge. Then there are those who believe and yet die. They are "called home" according to God's foreknowledge. Those who believe and survive, do so, because God is not yet finished with them and they still have a particular destiny to fulfill. They will be saved in the future, and are to be the parents and grandparents of offspring who will in the future believe and be saved—once again, all according to the foreknowledge of God.

I am not so presumptuous to think that I am able to offer an Adventist theodicy that will satisfy everyone and leave no loose ends. In fact, I do not believe any human being can explain how the reality of an infinitely powerful and loving God can coexist with the reality of evil and suffering. But I believe it is possible to maintain one's faith in God in spite of that tension. I hope the following remarks will at least help a few readers also to maintain their faith in God in spite of this dilemma. Please consider the following eight points:

### Evil is part of a larger picture

We may believe there is more than we hear, see, smell, and feel. Our faith may assure us that there is a God—one personal, yet triune, Being, who was before anything else was; the great absolute I AM, who is there for each and every one of us, always, totally, unconditionally. In addition, we may trust there are angels around us, even though most of us have never actually seen them. We may also believe the information given in God's Word that we are surrounded by evil forces—fallen angels in terrifying numbers. Many would further allow for the possibility that somewhere in the universe other forms of life and other intelligences exist. (Most would draw the line at reports about sightings of aliens or abductions of humans by visitors from outer space.) Nonetheless, for us human beings, our scope of vision remains largely limited to this earth.

Living on this earth we focus primarily on what we can perceive with our senses. Obviously, we are more concerned about what happens to us and our fellow-human beings than we are about what might be happening on other worlds in the universe, if such other worlds exist. And even when it comes to the things that happen on this earth, it is natural to be more concerned about those events that affect us or people we know and love than those events that affect people far away or whom we don't know. When a family member or a good friend happens to be in an area where a natural disaster strikes, our first question will be: Is he or she safe? We feel sorry for the thousands who lose their jobs when a large company in a neighboring town decides to downsize its operations, but it hits us much harder when our son or daughter is laid off. We are horrified by the pictures of AIDS victims in tropical Africa, but when someone we know tests HIV-positive, it becomes a totally different story. Every plane crash is terrible, but we pay special attention if we hear some Adventists were among the victims. We live in concentric circles, and what happens in the smallest circle affects us in a different, more personal, manner than what happens in the wider circles further away from us.

Therefore, thinking about the momentous questions related to evil and suffering, we must remember, first of all, our limited human perspective. We look at the smaller circles around us and cannot see the bigger picture as God, and He alone, can. That in itself should make us hesitant to suggest a human answer to the problem of suffering and to build a theodicy. We only see in part, only through "a poor reflection, as in a mirror" (1 Corinthians 13:12). British theologian Edward Vick reminds us that, when trying to understand something of divine providence, we must realize that there is a larger picture and that we must focus on the cosmic dimension rather than being content with a patchwork approach.[3]

### The mystery of evil

Where did evil come from? How could it suddenly emerge in a perfect universe? How could God allow it? And why did God not take firm measures when the first traces of evil were detected? The answer to each of these questions is: We do not know.

Of course, we find some information in the Bible. One passage in Isaiah and another in Ezekiel have a direct bearing on the origin of evil by referring to two ancient, godless kings as symbolic representations of the heavenly being that rebelled against God. Isaiah chapter 14 tells us that this heavenly being, referred to as the "morning star," the "son of the dawn," fell from his elevated position in heaven. Somehow, this being was no longer content with his status and said to himself, "I will ascend to heaven; I will raise my throne above the stars of God . . . I will make myself like the Most High" (verses 12-14).

Ezekiel 28 paints a similar picture. A being who was at one time "a guardian cherub . . . on the holy mount of God," and who was "blameless" in everything "from the day [he was] created" became proud and "wickedness was found in him" (verses 13-17).

The last book of the Bible adds some further details—the disease that began in heaven eventually infected the earth:

> And there was war in heaven. Michael and his angels fought against the dragon, and the dragon and his angels fought back. But he was not strong enough, and they lost their place in heaven. The great dragon was hurled down—that ancient serpent called the devil, or Satan, who leads the whole world astray. He was hurled to the earth, and his angels with him (Revelation 12:7-9).

What happened next is described in the story of our first ancestors. They fell into the trap of the devil, and the Garden of Eden became paradise lost. Sin had gained a foothold on this earth, and things would never be the same again until the day evil is finally eradicated and humanity will inherit a new earth, cleansed from sin.

Enough has been revealed to us to know that sin and all the misery that has followed in its tracks is foreign to God's original plans and purposes. Sin and suffering did not exist when God created everything out of nothing, and they will not exist when He makes "everything new" (Revelation 21:5). Sin and suffering, however, do exist very concretely and dramatically in this intermezzo between "paradise lost" and "paradise regained." That is all we know. However much we probe, we will not understand how evil could arise nor why God reacted to it the way He did. Ellen G. White puts it very succinctly:

> To many minds the origin of sin and the reason for its existence are a source of great perplexity. They see the work of evil, with its terrible results of woe and desolation, and they question how all this can exist under the sovereignty of One who is infinite in wisdom, in power, and in love. Here is a mystery of which they find no explanation. . . . It is impossible to explain the origin of sin so as to give a reason for its existence. Yet enough may be understood concerning both the origin and the final disposition of sin to make fully manifest the justice and benevolence of God in all His dealings with evil. Nothing is more plainly taught in Scripture than that God was in no way responsible for the entrance of sin; that there was no arbitrary withdrawal of divine grace, no deficiency in the divine government, that gave occasion for the uprising of rebellion. Sin is an intruder, for whose presence no reason can be given. It is mysterious, unaccountable; to excuse it is to defend it. Could excuse for it be found, or cause be shown for its existence, it would cease to be sin.[4]

**The risk of a free will**

God did not want to be served by robots and therefore gave His creatures, both angels and human beings, freedom of choice. Not a kind of make-believe freedom in which nothing could really go wrong. Real freedom to make real choices implies a definite risk. God took that calculated risk. Part of the heavenly beings made the wrong choice. That tragic fact did not diminish God in any way, but it transformed those angels into devils.

When Adam and Eve exercised their free will and made a conscious choice to disobey the divine instructions, their perfection and conditional immortality were replaced by imperfection and mortality, which they passed on to their offspring.

So, whatever we do, we must never blame God for the evil we see around us. It is not His choice; it is mankind's choice. And let us remember that the Divine decision to grant mankind freedom of choice also has its other side—we can choose to say "No" to sin and choose to accept the offer of wonderful grace that provides for an eternal way out.

Again, there are difficult issues to face. If man is truly free, can God know everything we are going to do even before we do it? If He is all-knowing, it seems that He must be able to do so. But if God knows everything from the beginning—if He knows what I am going to do before I do it—how can I be said to have free will? Does not God's foreknowledge suggest at least some degree of predestination? Are things not bound to go in predetermined ways if God knows all beforehand?

And what about prophecy? Are things set in concrete once a certain chain of events has been prophesied? Or could the exercise of free will still alter the outcome? Most answers to such questions would create new problems. It seems reasonable, however, to suggest that by granting His creatures freedom of choice at the risk of things going terribly wrong, God accepted a measure of self-limitation. He did not at any point relinquish part of His power, but His eternal love prompted Him to temporarily limit Himself in the exercise of that power, knowing as He did the larger picture.

### Limited freedom

The fact that our freedom is a real freedom does not imply that it is unlimited freedom. We are born at a particular point in time, in a particular country, in a particular home. The fact that I was born in 1942 (rather than in 1842), in the Netherlands (rather than in Russia), in a working-class family (rather than as the son of a rich banker) has provided me with innumerable options, but these realities have also excluded many possibilities. Each of us has a certain genetic make-up that we cannot (yet) change. In spite of a healthful lifestyle, the genetic make-up that we have inherited from our parents may sharply increase the chance that we will die from a particular disease.

Some decisions made early in life can never be undone. Things we would desperately like to do may forever remain beyond our reach, simply because we once made a particular choice.

But there is something even more troublesome. We are often pulled in a direction we do not want to go. The apostle Paul acknowledged that he was subject to some extremely strong urges: "For what I want to do I do not do, but what I hate I do" (Romans 7:15).

Something is fundamentally wrong with the human race. Often this predicament is referred to as "original sin." Many have a totally wrong idea of what "original sin" is, but this is not the place to discuss the concept in any depth. In the context of this chapter, we should note, however, that our present freedom is limited by the history of the human race, by this constant pull in the wrong direction. This side of the Kingdom, perfection is not within our reach!

This brings us to the next point: We are responsible for our own free choices, but not for the things we cannot change. Sin has caused havoc in all areas of life, but we are not *personally* responsible for everything that has gone wrong and that may yet go wrong in the future. Natural disasters are, indirectly but undeniably, the result of sin, but in most cases we do not bear any personal responsibility for them. I cannot, by exercising my power of free choice, prevent a volcano from erupting, but I can decide to assist some of the victims by sending a check to the Red Cross. I do not bear any direct responsibility for the atrocities committed in the constant wars in Africa nor for the dreadful colonial past that goes a long way toward explaining many of today's woes. But I can use my free choice in doing everything I can to push for reconciliation in the organization in which I work and in the environment in which I live. The terrible inequality between rich and poor is definitely linked to sin. But I do not need to take the whole world on my shoulders and feel guilty if I enjoy some of the good things of life. I am, on the other hand, responsible and *should* feel guilty if I fail to help those who cross my path.

God has given us the gift of free will. He does not expect us to change the whole world. He will do that for us when His time has come. But He does expect us to use this precious gift within the limits of our situation. Unfortunately, our first parents made a wrong choice and, ever since, men and women have continued to make wrong choices. At times, our wrong decisions increase the misery for ourselves and others. But the alternative, being automatons without freedom of choice, would be infinitely worse.

**Suffering and sin**

There is a definite link between sin and suffering. Sometimes the connection is abundantly clear. People who smoke two packs of cigarettes a day should not be amazed if they end up with emphysema or lung cancer. People who disregard all laws of healthful living must expect the dire consequences. Having unprotected sex with many different partners is not only morally objectionable, but is also an extremely risky business that may well prove fatal.

In these and many other cases, there is clearly a direct link between our behavior or decisions and the suffering that follows. Bad things happen to bad people. What worries us, though, is that bad things do not happen only to them. Bad things also happen to good people!

Anyone with a little knowledge of the Bible will know that there is a book in the Old Testament dedicated to the problem of suffering. It tells the story of Job, a fabulously rich sheik in the patriarchal age, who all of a sudden falls victim to a series of unparalleled disasters. The first few chapters make clear that Job is not struck by bad luck or blind fate. The author introduces us to a court scene in heaven; the key players are God and His angels, Satan and his troops, and Job. Job is described as "blameless and upright; he feared God and shunned evil" (Job 1:1). But Satan claims that Job's piety is rooted in his self-interest. "Take his wealth away from him," he suggests, "and Job will be a different man." The gist of the story is that God allows Satan to envelop Job with misery. He gets a free hand, as long as he spares Job's life.

True to his reputation, Satan appears to be highly efficient in his destructive work. Job loses everything he has—his possessions, his children, the respect of his wife, and even his health. In chapter 2:7 we find him "afflicted with painful sores from the soles of his feet to the top of his head." And we are told: "Then Job took a piece of broken pottery and scraped himself with it as he sat among the ashes" (verse 8).

The story continues. Job's friends arrive to comfort him in his troubles.

With such friends, Job needs no further enemies! They claim to know why Job suffers—he is guilty of some sin. In particular, Job's friend Eliphaz points out, none too subtly, that Job must have been involved in some secret vice. What other reason could there be for his distress?

Throughout history people have made this direct connection between sin and suffering. If someone suffers, there must be a reason! If she is in trouble, it must somehow be her own fault! This was a common perception in Christ's day. As Jesus "went along, He saw a man blind from birth." His disciples asked him, " 'Rabbi, who sinned, this man or his parents, that he was born blind?' " (John 9:1).

Note that the disciples' immediate thought was that the blindness was somehow caused by sin. The only question they had was whether it was the sin of the blind man himself or the sins of his parents that had caused the blindness. Jesus does not go along with that kind of reasoning. He does not deny that somehow the occurrence of blindness in this world is the result of sin. But He does not want to hear of a direct link between a particular sin of this man or of his parents and the fact that he could not see. Christ puts the whole incident in a larger framework: " 'Neither this man nor his parents sinned . . . but this happened so that the work of God might be displayed in his life' " (verse 2).

In Luke 13:1-5, the same point is made in possibly an even more dramatic way. In these verses, Jesus receives a report about atrocities committed by Pilate against some Galileans, and then asks the question that must have been on many minds: " 'Do you think that these Galileans were worse sinners than all the other Galileans because they suffered this way?' " Jesus answers His own question: " 'I tell you, no!' " He then refers to another incident and repeats the point: " 'Or those eighteen who died when the tower in Siloam fell on them—do you think they were more guilty than all the others living in Jerusalem?' " Again, the emphatic answer is: " 'I tell you, no! But unless you repent, you too will all perish.' "

Although there is a link between sin and suffering, there is not necessarily a connection between a specific mishap and a specific sin. If only we could see the larger picture, we would not come to such superficial conclusions as did

Job's friends or Jesus' disciples.

There is also something else to consider: It may sometimes seem as if we are constantly bombarded by adversity. But there is another side which we usually fail to take into account. Were it not for God's constant gracious intervention on our behalf, we would have ceased to exist long ago. The moments when disaster strikes are, in fact, the exceptions and not the rule. As a rule, we are protected. Only occasionally, as the divine protection is withdrawn, does misery strike. If we would just remember this, it would place our afflictions in a different perspective.

**No easy answers**

If the story of Job teaches us anything, it is that there are no easy answers to the question of why people suffer or to the related question of why some "good" people suffer so many bad things, while some really "bad" people seem to have all the fun and the luck in the world.

Some may think that they have worked out a reasonably satisfying theodicy that gives due attention to God's power and His love, on the one hand, and to our free will on the other. But have they really? If there were only a moderate amount of suffering, it might make some sense to argue that God, seeing the larger picture, is willing to allow for a certain amount of misery. We might, for instance, be able to accept the reasonableness of sickness and death of adults, but can we ever come to terms with the premature death of a child?

It has often been remarked that it is not just the existence of evil and suffering that is so hard to take, but it is the sheer *quantity* of suffering, the terrible scale of death and destruction, the total depravity of so many, and the terrible wickedness that is so widespread, that is so utterly problematic.

Moreover, some may feel that they have arrived at an intellectually satisfying conclusion in their quest for the "why" of suffering. But will their conclusions remain convincing when they themselves are faced with terrible pain and relentless suffering?

The book of Job points us in the direction of a different kind of solution—one that is experiential rather than intellectual. The final chapters describe an encounter between Job and God. It is a powerful word picture of the untiring divine attempt to make Job, and us, realize that we see only a few pieces of the puzzle. But the one and only true Creator-God sees the larger picture. Whatever happens, He continues to care for us. He is still in control, regardless of external appearances that may suggest otherwise. When we are at the end of our tether, our first concern must not be to understand, but to trust. Job learned the lesson we all must learn. He finally saw that He needed a deeper relationship with God. He knew *about* God, but He did not really *know Him* in a personal way. Once he came to that new stage in his experience, the "why" question and the false solutions of his friends ceased to have the same urgency they had before. Now Job knew his place before the Almighty God, in whose hands he could safely commit all his troubles. " 'My ears had heard of you,' " he said to God, " 'but now my eyes have seen you' " (Job 42:5).

Accepting the fact that pain and suffering are realities of present life and that somehow they fit into God's larger picture, does not mean that we should welcome misery. Quite often Christians have believed that self-inflicted suffering is pleasing in God's sight. There is, however, absolutely nothing in the Bible to support the idea that God enjoys human mortification or a good dose of godly masochism. Christians are to relieve suffering wherever they can, and not to promote it as a spiritual exercise. If we are suffering, we should ask God for strength to endure our pain. And we should ask Him to open our eyes, so that we can discern evil wherever it exists, and plead with Him for the courage to combat it in whatever way we can.

### The bright side of suffering

Bad things remain bad things, but they can have positive side effects. Suffering can make us stronger and better persons. Some learn to swear when they suffer, but for others suffering becomes an avenue of spiritual growth. This is particularly true when we are made to suffer for sticking to the principles we believe in. Remember the words of the apostle Peter; they are also addressed to us:

> Dear friends, do not be surprised at the painful trial you are suffering, as though something strange were happening to you. But

> rejoice that you participate in the sufferings of Christ, so that you may be overjoyed when his glory is revealed. If you are insulted because of the name of Christ, you are blessed, for the Spirit of glory and of God rests on you (1 Peter 4:12-14).

Jesus said the very same thing in His Sermon on the Mount, when He stated, " 'Blessed are you when people insult you, persecute you and falsely say all kinds of evil against you because of me' " (Matthew 5:11). And Paul left no doubt that he saw the many life-threatening events that had marked his career as occasions for spiritual growth. "When I am weak, then I am strong," he said (2 Corinthians 12:10).

Paul's testimony is not unique. Many have experienced spiritual growth and have become more mature, more caring and better people as the result of the suffering they have undergone. Recently I read about Bob Buford, a former business tycoon who decided to change the direction of his life at "half time."[5] Today he heads a support ministry for pastors and church leaders. How did he find the strength and courage to take stock of his life and make a new start? In early 1987 his son, Ross, just one year out of college and already successful as an investment banker, drowned while swimming in the Rio Grande River that separates south Texas from Mexico. The Texas Rangers started an intense search, and father Bob hired airplanes, helicopters, boats, trackers with dogs—everything that money could buy. Four months later, Ross's body was found. It was the end of Ross's life, but the beginning of a new life for his father Bob.

> As horrifying and sad as it was, and is, to have lost him, Ross' disappearance and death also provided the greatest moments of rare insight and the grandest gestures of immeasurable grace and joy that I ever hope to experience. Utter emptiness and brokenness left me feeling awful and wonderful at the same time. Close and silent embraces from friends, letters and phone calls of concern and empathy, and gifts of meals prepared and brought to our home were much-needed signs of love.

5—O.A.G.

Just days after the funeral Bob Buford was able to pray, "God, You have given my life into my hands. I give it back to You. My time, my property, my life itself . . . knowing it is only an instant compared to my life with You in eternity."[6]

Some time ago, I read of another example of someone whose life was greatly enriched by the ordeal he had to experience. Bas van Iersel, the former chancellor of a Dutch university, had been suffering from cancer for more than twenty-five years. A number of times he thought he would not survive, but he did, having one remission after the other. A few years ago, he said in a television interview that his illness never made him doubt God's love for him. He explained that it had changed his life and made him truly thankful for every new day. To the surprise of his friends he threw a big party twenty-five years after the day he was first diagnosed with cancer. "Some people," he said, "thought that I was crazy. Who would want to celebrate a quarter of a century of illness?" But van Iersel had learned to see things from a different perspective. His God had added twenty-five years to his life! What better reason could one have to throw a party?[7]

**The only answer: Jesus Christ**

We are left with many questions, and at the end of the chapter we may still find it difficult to give a solid response to Lactantius. But whatever questions we may continue to have, we should never allow ourselves to doubt God's love. The fact that He allows evil to run its course (at least to some degree, because if He did not drastically curtail it, none of us would be here to ask any questions!), does not mean that His love for us is less than perfect.

When we are perplexed by the "why" of the misery of this world, we must focus on the event that took place almost two thousand years ago on a Friday afternoon on a hill near Jerusalem. In His inscrutable way of dealing with the sin problem in all its cosmic dimensions, God decided to become one with us in His Son, Jesus Christ. For more than thirty years Jesus shared in our human existence in a manner we shall never understand. "He emptied Himself," the apostle Paul stated in an attempt to put the essence of the miracle of the Incarnation into human words (Philippians 2:8; KJV, margin). And He went all the way "even to death on the cross." How can anyone legitimately doubt the love of Someone who gives Himself so totally, so unreservedly? Should we not step back in awe and grateful admiration for a love "so amazing, so divine," rather than to keep harboring doubts when we feel that God remains silent in the midst of our suffering? Edward Vick puts it as follows:

> When no voice comes to answer the questions that press for attention, it may be that God provides the means thereby of asking whether *the* important question has not already been answered. Through Christ's cross, light may fall in unexpected ways upon puzzlements and doubts.
>
> The cross, the worst man can do, does not overpower God's goodness. The evil of the world is taken up by Him and made the instrument of His redemptive purpose. If that can be done here—and to the Son of God—it is possible to believe that nothing can stand in final opposition to the will that found its expression here. Thus the final answer to the problem is one of faith and experience.[8]

Few people have seen the identification of a loving and compassionate God with human suffering as clearly as Auschwitz and Buchenwald-survivor and Nobel Peace Prize winner Elie Wiesel. The book *Night* is the terrifying account of Wiesel's experience as a young Jewish boy in a Nazi death camp. Ten years after his deliverance from the camp, he felt finally able to write about it. One of the most hair-raising and yet touching passages describes how the Gestapo decided to hang three persons—two adults and a young boy—to take revenge for an act of sabotage by some camp inmates. The two adults were the first to die.

> But the third rope was still moving; being so light, the child was still alive . . . For more than half an hour he stayed there, struggling between life and death, dying in slow agony under our eyes. And we had to look him full in the face. He was still alive when I passed in front of him. His tongue was still red, his eyes were not yet glazed.

# OUR AWESOME GOD

Behind me, I heard [a] man asking: "Where is God now?"

And I heard a voice within me answer him "Where is He? Here He is—He is hanging here on the gallows."[9]

---

[1] Quoted in: Dominique Morin, *How to Understand God*?, (London: SMC Press, 1990), 87.

[2] *Ibid.*, 89.

[3] Edward Vick, *Speaking Well of God* (Nashville, Tenn.: Southern Publishing Association, 1979), 175.

[4] Ellen G. White, *The Great Controversy*, 492.

[5] See his book *Half Time: Changing your Game Plan from Success to Significance* (Grand Rapids, Mich.: Zondervan Publishing House, 1994).

[6] *Ibid.*, 54-60.

[7] *Ik Geloof: Mensen Praten over God* (Baarn: Gooi & Sticht, 1993), 45-47.

[8] Vick, 176.

[9] Elie Wiesel, *Night* (New York: Bantam Books, 1982 ed.), 62.

**Chapter Ten**

# Is Allah God?

Why does the Seventh-day Adventist Church put so much of its energy and resources into missions? For most church members the answer is rather obvious: The gospel must be preached to those who have not yet heard of the Christian God and of what He has done in Jesus Christ. And the Adventist message must be brought to those who have not come into full discipleship and who, so far, have not accepted all implications of biblical truth. The gospel commission is clear:

> "Therefore go and make disciples of all nations, baptizing them in the name of the Father and of the Son and of the Holy Spirit, and teaching them to obey everything I have commanded you. And surely I am with you always, to the very end of the age" (Matthew 28:19, 20).

How much clearer can it be? The corporate church, as well as the individual believer, has the duty to share the faith, wherever and whenever possible. All people must hear the Good News. And God has decided to use us human beings to announce His offer of grace. We must go and find those who do not yet believe, for "how can they [people] believe in the one of whom they have not heard? And how can they hear without someone preaching to them?" (Romans 10:14).

It seems strange that something so obvious would be so hotly debated by so many of today's theologians. Yet that is very much the case.

**How much knowledge is needed for salvation?**

Today, most Adventists no longer believe that they are the only ones who will be saved. Those who are still of that opinion (and some, unfortunately, see things that way), do so despite the official belief of their church. Yet, only a generation or so ago it was quite generally accepted among Adventists that anyone who had had the opportunity to hear the Adventist message but who had not joined the "remnant church," would inevitably face eternal loss as a consequence. Moreover, many church members believed they would put their own salvation at considerable risk by deviating from even one of the doctrines of the Adventist truth. I still remember (I must have been about twelve at the time) my mother discussing some obscure prophetic detail with another church member and I recall how horrified this member was when my mother ventured to suggest that one's understanding of such matters did not necessarily affect one's salvation!

Today, many Seventh-day Adventists recognize that they do not have a monopoly on the Christian faith. We recognize that there are sincere believers in other Protestant churches and even in the Roman Catholic Church! These sincere believers will be saved, most Adventists would say in their precious jargon, "as long as they live according to the light they have received," and as long as "before the end of time" they make the decision to join "the remnant church." Adventists clearly recognize that, although some of their beliefs differ in significant ways from those of other sincere Christians, all Christians basically serve the same triune God whom they have encountered as Father, Son, and Holy Spirit. Adventists accept the fact that all sincere Christians are candidates for heaven.

What, though, about those who are Christians in name only, but who do not know God in any experiential way? What about those who are so liberal in their theological views that their God can no longer be recognized as the one and only true Christian God, as a Person to whom we can relate and who has revealed Himself in Jesus Christ? Can such people be saved for eternity in spite of the absence of a commitment to the God of the Bible?

What about the approximately three billion non-Christians alive today? Can they be saved if they die before someone has reached them with the message of the Christian God? Or is their only hope for eternity in fully accepting the biblical doctrines of God, Christ, salvation, etc.? And is eternal loss their inevitable future if they do not hear and respond to the Christian message?

### Inclusivists or exclusivists?

Those who have given thought to these and similar questions can be divided into "inclusivists" and "exclusivists."

The inclusivists believe that God reveals Himself in all religious traditions, and that all religions can, therefore, be avenues to salvation. They point to the many similarities between Christianity and other religions and to the positive aspects of non-Christian religions. They commend Islam for its high moral concepts, eastern religions for their emphasis on contemplation, and even discern some embryonic Christian notions in the African traditional religions (which most Christians used to refer to as simply paganism). A number of prominent Christian theologians, John H. Hick and Paul F. Knitter, for example, enthusiastically promote the idea of inclusivism.

But the exclusivists are adamantly opposed to this line of thinking. They agree that there are superficial similarities between Christianity and other religions but insist that there are also fundamental differences. They argue that the truth claims of the various religions cannot be ignored. Opposing beliefs cannot all simultaneously be true. Some, at least, are untrue and must therefore be rejected.

Christianity, they say, is unique because Christ is unique. Whatever other religions may have to offer, they do not have Christ, and He is precisely what all human beings need. Speaking of Christ, the apostle Peter declared, "Salvation is found in no one else, for there is no other name under heaven given to men by which we must be saved" (Acts 4:12). Paul agreed wholeheartedly. "For there is one God and one mediator between God and men, the man Christ Jesus" (1 Timothy 2:5).

If we take the Bible seriously, we must line up with the exclusivists. Ellen G. White probably never heard the term "exclusivist," but she surely belonged to that school of thought.

> In all ages, philosophers and teachers have been presenting to the world theories by which to satisfy the soul's need. Every heathen nation has had its great teachers and religious systems offering some other means of redemption than Christ, turning the eyes of men away from the Father's face, and filling their hearts with fear of Him who has given them only blessing. . . . It is the gospel of the grace of God alone that can uplift the soul. The contemplation of the love of God manifested in His Son will stir the heart and arouse the powers of the soul as nothing else can.[1]

Salvation is only through Christ. That does not automatically mean that those who have never heard of Christ cannot be saved. After all, God's people in Old Testament times had not heard of Jesus Christ, and they were offered salvation! It does mean, however, that if some of those are ultimately saved who have never heard of Christ, but who have lived according to their conscience and in accordance with what they know to be right, it will be only because Jesus Christ has provided their entrance ticket into heaven. Whether people know it or not, if they are going to be saved, it is only because God gave His Son also for them.

### We must go, that others may hear

The fact that some (or even many) of those who have only a rudimentary knowledge of God's plan of salvation (or even none at all) may nonetheless reach heaven, does not diminish the urgency of telling as many people as possible, and as quickly as possible, about the God who in His love has reached out to us through His Son and who is ever with us through His Spirit.

If God wants us to go, preach, teach, and make disciples for Him, these activities must obviously make a difference to the people "out there." God would not ask us to be His ambassadors if it did not serve some essential function. Apparently, people may be lost if they are not reached in time with the gospel.

I have often wondered about the fairness of having someone's eternal destiny depend on the loyalty of God's people to the gospel commission. But at long last I have decided not to worry about this any more. I must trust God that His plan is totally fair. I must trust in His righteous love—or should I say in His loving justice?—that guarantees no one will be lost without having had some real opportunity or some kind of choice. I must believe that God alone sees the larger picture, and therefore that He has a solid reason for His determination to use us human beings as His agents to tell the world of His divine rescue package.

Mission, therefore, remains an imperative. Those who know about God must share their knowledge of Him. By itself, however, that would be an inadequate basis for missionary work. It could easily become merely a burdensome duty. But when we know the one and only true God, when we have met Him and find joy in talking with Him, listening to Him, and worshiping Him—sharing that experiential knowledge of Him will not be an unpleasant burden but a privilege of sheer joy. The wording may be somewhat dated, but the thoughts Ellen White expressed in the paragraph below are as relevant and applicable today as they were when first written more than a century ago:

> Angels of God are waiting, desiring with intense desire that those who claim to believe the truth shall become agents through which, by co-operation with them, they shall be able to communicate light to the world. All heaven is interested in the

> work that is going on in the world, and the angels desire that men shall become channels by which divine grace may flow to those who are famishing for the waters of life. In new and fresh aspects the truth is to be presented through living agencies to those who are in the darkness of error, who are dead in trespasses and sins. . . . The salvation of the human soul is the one object of most intense interest to the heavenly host. The value of the soul is infinitely above silver and gold; and why is it that you who have a knowledge of the truth do not impart it to others?. . . . Go to work to save souls that are ready to perish. Personal effort must be put forth, if men who are lost are to be convinced that they are in need of a Saviour. . . . To every man God has given his work. Every soul that has been enlightened has a work to do, a mission to perform.[2]

**But what about the God of the Jews and the Muslims?**

Before leaving this topic we need to look at one further aspect. There is no escape from the conclusion that those who do not know the one and only Almighty God who created heaven and earth, and who reaches out to us with infinite love, must be told of Him. Without knowing this God, all religion remains idol worship. But what about the Jews and the Muslims? I am here using these terms in a rather loose sense, realizing that just as there are many kinds of Christians, there are also wide variations in religious conviction and commitment among Jews and Muslims.

Christianity, Judaism, and Islam are usually bundled together as the three monotheistic religions, as indeed they are. Many historical and conceptual ties bind these three world religions together. Christians, Jews, and Muslims all regard Abraham as a common ancestor. They believe in one God who is the Creator of everything. They share a similar view of time and believe that history, as we now know it, will end by an act of divine intervention. They share a common body of ethical principles, and all three attach great importance to holy writings.[3]

The God-concept of Jews and Muslims has a strong resemblance to the God who is presented in the Old Testament. Therefore, there is no doubt that Jews and Muslims possess extensive knowledge of the one and only true God. But one might say that their view of God has been frozen in time.

For a moment, let's focus on the Muslim view of God in particular. While there are now only some fifteen million Jews in the world—and only a minority of these is serious about the traditional Jewish religion—there are almost one billion Muslims. From our perspective, Muslims used to live mostly in "far-away places," but today millions of them have come to live in the Western world and have come to stay, as the hundreds of new mosques that spring up everywhere clearly indicate. A considerable percentage of Muslims does not fully practice the Muslim faith, but hundreds of millions do.

Who is the "Allah" who is worshiped by so many people? The name *Allah* should not be a problem to Christians. *Allah* is the standard Arabic word for *God*, and the word is used by Arab Christians as well as by Muslims. The Muslim Allah and the Christian God have much in common. In the Koran, a number of themes dominate—Allah is the Creator, the Judge, and the Rewarder; He is unique and inherently One; and He is omnipotent and all-merciful. He is the "Lord of the Worlds," the Most High, and "nothing is like unto Him." Allah has a multitude of names, but—and this is crucial—allusions to His love are conspicuously absent. The response of the Muslim worshiper, in turn, is primarily one of obedience and submission rather than of love.

The Christian God is personal, loving, concerned, and holy, while the Muslim sees Allah as distant, almighty, and merciful—yet capricious and vengeful.[4]

### Jesus Christ

Muslims do know about Jesus, or "Isa" as they call Him. But they do not recognize Him as God or as their Savior. For them, He is an important prophet among many other prophets. For the Christian, the very mention of Jesus Christ immediately evokes a mental picture of self-sacrificing love, of total, unconditional identification with mankind. The Muslim, on the other hand, greets the name of Christ with ambivalence. He appreciates the life and ministry of Jesus and sees Him as one of the great prophets. But, at the same time "there are cynicism and disgust over the fact that around this man has risen [what the Muslim considers to be] a cult of deity worship."[5] The Muslim, in other words, respects Jesus the prophet, but despises Christ the Lord.

From time to time one hears suggestions that Adventists should find it easier than other Christians to "win" Muslims because of some significant similarities in lifestyle between Adventism and Islam. But let us not make the fundamental mistake of thinking that just because we share the same view on such things as refusing to eat pork means that Adventists are significantly closer to Muslims than are Baptists or Catholics. The key issue is: Christians believe in a God who revealed Himself in Christ; Muslims do not.

It is often pointed out that, just as Christianity has Christ, other religions have their own religious figures. And, indeed, we must have great respect for Mohammed, who courageously condemned idolatry and insisted on the worship of one God in a highly polytheistic society. And for the Gautama Buddha's compassion and sensitivity to human suffering, as well as for the profound teachings of Confucius. But these religious figures do not begin to compare with Jesus Christ.

Christ is absolutely unique. No other founder of a major religion has had the audacity to claim to be the eternal Creator. No other religious figure has claimed to be able to forgive sin. Jesus died, like all other religious figures, but He was the only One to be resurrected! "To suggest, then, that Jesus and the other religious leaders are essentially in the same category is to play fast and loose with what the New Testament says about Jesus. Jesus is unique."[6]

The God Christians must proclaim to the world is the God who has come to this world in Jesus Christ. Jews and Muslims know of the God of Abraham, Isaac, and Jacob, but then they come to a full stop. They have refused to accept the glorious self-revelation of God in His

Son, Jesus Christ. Therefore, though we must be ready to acknowledge that Jews, Muslims, and Christians begin at the same point, we must also be totally clear about the fact that Jews and Muslims are on a track that differs fundamentally from "the Way" (Acts 9:2) of the Christian. They know important things *about* God, but they do not *know* God to the extent that He can be known. They are missing out on the most important part.

It would, therefore, be improper to say that Jews and Muslims do not worship the same God as do Christians. But, at the same time, Christians must insist that the Jewish and the Islamic concepts of God are truncated concepts, to put it mildly. In their own distinct ways, Jews and Muslims have remained at a preliminary stage in the search for God, and they desperately need to come to a fuller understanding of how God has revealed Himself in Jesus Christ.

That is why the Christian mission to the Jews and to the Muslims remains such a unique challenge. In spite of all the distrust, hatred and even bloodshed that has existed among them, there is also a bond uniting the adherents of the three monotheistic world religions. But Jews and Muslims must hear and accept the Good News that Christ has come into the world as "God with us" (Matthew 1:23). They must focus on Him and realize that God was indeed in our midst and that in an unparalleled way, He represents all that God stands for.

> Justice and mercy are the attributes of [God's] throne. He is a God of love, of pity, and tender compassion. Thus He is represented in his Son, our Saviour. He is a God of patience and long-suffering. If such is the being whom we adore, and whose character we are seeking to imitate, we are worshipping the true God.[7]

Do Jews and Muslims know the one and only true God? As long as they do not know Him as the Father-Son-Holy Spirit God, they know Him, at best, from a distance. Their worship may be genuine and sincere, but it is not the kind of worship with which God can be satisfied.

Humanity's approach to God is through Jesus. There is no other way.

---

[1] Ellen G. White, *The Desire of Ages*, 478.
[2] Ellen G. White, *Advent Review and Sabbath Herald*, 12 December, 1993.
[3] Hans Kung, *Credo—The Apostles' Creed Explained for Today* (London: SCM Press, 1993), 14.
[4] David J. Hesselgrave, *Communicating Christ Cross-Culturally* (Grand Rapids, Mich.: Zondervan Publishing House, 1978), 186.
[5] Phil Parshall, *New Paths in Muslim Evangelism* (Grand Rapids, Mich.: Baker Book House, 1980), 75, 76.
[6] Harold A. Netland, *Dissonant Voices: Religious Pluralism and the Question of Truth.* (Grand Rapids: William B. Eerdmans Publishing Co, 1991), 260-262.
[7] Ellen G. White, 'The Privileges and Duties of the Followers of Christ', *Advent Review and Sabbath Herald*, March 12, 1908.

## Chapter Eleven

# Reflecting God

In this book we have been looking at God. It is now time, perhaps, to look at ourselves. If God is so almighty, so good, so full of righteousness and justice, and so awesome in His love and compassion—where does that leave us? We cannot help but have great sympathy for the prophet Isaiah, who, when confronted with the glory and majesty of God, cried out: "Woe to me!. . . I am ruined! For I am a man of unclean lips, and I live among a people of unclean lips, and my eyes have seen the King, the Lord Almighty" (Isaiah 6:5).

How does the Bible respond to our deep sense of unworthiness in the presence of our Maker? It tells us, first of all, never to lose our sense of perspective: We were "formed" from "the dust of the ground" (Genesis 2:7). God still "remembers that we are dust," and that "As for man, his days are like grass, he flourishes like a flower of the field; the wind blows over it and it is gone, and its place remembers it no more" (Psalm 103:14-16). But the very same psalm (Psalm 103) adds something very significant: God's "love is with those who fear Him." Human beings are not much in themselves, but they are, nevertheless, special in God's eyes.

God gave us a unique status. He made us just "a little lower than the heavenly beings and crowned [us]. . . with glory and honor." (Psalm 8:5; see also Hebrews 2:7). All that God created He said was "good" (Genesis 1:4,10,12,18, 21). But when He had finished creating the first human being, He described His handiwork as "very good" (Genesis 1:31). One specific aspect is mentioned to explain why the man was "very good"—he was created in the "image of God" (Genesis 1:27).

Before we try to summarize in contemporary language what it means to be created in the image of God, we need to survey briefly the relevant biblical data. The key text is Genesis 1:27: "So God created man in His own image, in the image of God He created him; male and female He created them." The statement is repeated in Genesis 5:1 in the introduction to the genealogies recorded in that chapter, and in Genesis 9:6, when, immediately after the flood, God addresses Noah and reminds him that hurting a human being means touching a creature made in the image of God. Many centuries later, the apostle James warns the readers of his short letter that it is wrong to curse one's fellow humans, since they are made "in the likeness of God" (James 3:9).

What happened to this *imago Dei* when sin entered the world? We have already seen how this foreign element in God's perfect universe played havoc with nature in general and with mankind in particular. Humans became subject to degeneration, disease, and death. Adam's impeccable sense of morality was replaced by a constantly nagging temptation to pursue evil rather than good. But though scratched and damaged, the image of God was never totally defaced.

Because of the consequences of sin, however, human beings have need of a full restoration of this divine image. We must "put on the new self, created to be like God in true righteousness and holiness" (Ephesians 4:24). Our spiritual goal is to come to the point that "with unveiled faces [we] all reflect the Lord's glory", as we "are being transformed into [God's] likeness with ever-increasing glory" (2 Corinthians 3:18).

As always, Christ is our example and anchor-point; we are His followers. He is "the image of the invisible God" (Colossians 1:15), or as the author of the letter to the Hebrews puts it, He is "the radiance of

God's glory and the exact representation of His being" (Hebrews 1:3). That is our point of reference.

Often, in heated discussions about the origin of life on this earth, and of human life in particular, people fail to recognize the deeper meaning of what it means that God is the Creator and that we, human beings, are creatures, made "in the image of God." Yet, this is the focal point of the Creation story. The Genesis story wants us to realize that not only are we created beings, but we are God's special agents, created in His image. Although He is totally different, in a class of His own, yet in some paradoxical way, we do resemble Him.

The fact that we are made in God's image confers on us a tremendous dignity. If ever there was an argument against slavery or discrimination, this is it. How can one being, created in God's image, dare to ignore that divine image in a fellow human being?

On the one hand, we should never deny or trivialize the reality of sin. But on the other hand, we should also never lose sight of God's immeasurable greatness and the infinite distance between God, the Creator, and humans, the creatures. One thing should always be clear—being created in God's image does not mean that we are a fragment of the divine. To believe that would be to succumb to pantheism.[1] But, likewise, we should never forget how God has underscored our human dignity. John Macquarrie, a British theology professor, hits the nail on the head when he writes, "If we depreciate man, we drag down God with him, for in so doing we lessen the wonder of God's creation."

Among the many statements Ellen G. White made about the "image of God" that man received at creation, the following is one of the most concise (and provides a useful bridge to the next section of this chapter):

> God said, "Let us make man in our image." He gave to the work of His hands not only a form resembling His own, but a mind capable of comprehending divine things. His understanding, His memory, His imagination,—every faculty of man's mind,—reflected the image of God. In disposition and heart he was

> qualified to receive heavenly instruction. He possessed a right understanding, a true knowledge of his Creator, of himself, his duty, his obligations in respect to the law of God. His judgment was uncorrupted, unbiased, and disposed to obedience and affection, regulated according to reason and truth. He was capable of enjoying to the utmost capacity the good gifts of God. Everything upon which he looked was transporting to his senses; every sound was as music in his ears. Yet he was not placed beyond the reach of temptation. He stood as the representative of the human race,—a free moral agent.[2]

In all honesty, I must confess that this statement from Mrs. White's pen contains one very puzzling element. As a matter of fact, it is also found in scores of similar statements she made over the years. She seems to suggest that human beings somehow resemble God in a *physical* way; that there is a likeness in *form*. I wonder what she could have meant by that. Throughout her writings, she portrays God as a spiritual, infinite, and omnipresent Being. In speaking of God, she often employs the same kind of anthropomorphic language as does the Bible, that is, she regularly describes God in human terms, as having a mouth, ears, a heart, arms, and hands. But no one who reads the Bible in its entirety can be left with the impression that God has a human form. He is "Spirit," Christ Himself tells us (John 4:24). Therefore, when Ellen White seems to imply that God has a body to which our bodies bear a resemblance, I believe we must not rush to conclusions, but must be careful to balance such statements against her overall portrayal of God. We must not infer from these statements about a similarity in "form" that God has some kind of material body of which our bodies are a reflection. When I meet Mrs. White I hope to ask her about this. In any case, my view of her inspiration can accommodate this type of difficulty.

The other elements of the statement quoted above correspond closely to what has been the traditional understanding of the image of God in man—"a mind capable of comprehending divine things. . . [man's] understanding, his memory, his imagination,—every faculty of man's mind."

Some have emphasized human reason, will, or personality as the essence of the divine image. They point to the capacity of human beings to think abstractly and to make use of symbols. Others believe God's image in humanity has primarily to do with our capacity to build and maintain relationships. Still others believe the image of God is something which a person does. Immediately after God made Adam and Eve in His image, He gave them authority to "rule" over the whole earth (Genesis 1:28). According to this view, the active tending and caring for God's creation seems to constitute the image of God in man. Others argue that God's image is especially manifest in the fact that unlike the animals, human beings are not limited to basic instincts, but have the power of free choice. Some would say that human sexuality is at least one aspect of this *imago Dei.* (The Genesis context would suggest that this is a valid point. Genesis 1:27 reads: "God created man in his own image, in the *image of God* He created him; *male and female* He created them" [emphasis supplied]. The wording would indicate that something in the maleness and female-ness of humanity is part of the divine image.)

Rather than focusing on just one aspect however, it seems safe to suggest that all these elements, and many others, are part of what it means to be created in God's image. But some points, I believe, merit special attention.

### Responsible beings

We are not here by chance; we exist because God wanted to populate this planet with human beings bearing His image. Some of us may not have been wanted by our parents, but God wanted every one of us. That fact, in itself, should give a transcendent meaning to our lives.

There is, however, another side to the coin. Our creatureliness also presents us with definite boundaries. We are only creatures, and we should therefore know our place. We are not the Creator and should never behave as if we were. With Isaiah we must humbly confess: "O Lord, you are our Father. We are the clay, you are the potter; we are all the work of your hand" (Isaiah 64:8).

Standing as finite creatures before an infinite Creator confers a great responsibility on us. In this case we must go to the root meaning of the word *responsible*—our responsibility is that we must *respond.* In spite of our sinful state, we have retained the ability to respond to God's communications to us. Ever since God called our first ancestors with the words " 'Where are you?' " (Genesis 3:9), He has been repeating that same question, over and over again, in the life of every single human being who has ever lived. Even today, He wants to know where we are, whether we are running away from Him or searching for Him. As creatures, we have the choice; we must respond, one way or the other.

### Creativity

It is significant that the issue of the image of God is brought to our attention in the context of the Creation story. To me, this clearly suggests that creativity is a key element of this divine image. God is presented as the Creator (capital C), and we bear His image! We therefore are also creators (small c). We are endowed with gifts and talents. God made us, not as automatons who can perform a few movements that have been programmed into us through a built-in chip, but as creative beings. We can enjoy beautiful things and possess, or can develop, artistic abilities. God, the Master Artist, wants us to work in His workshop. He wants us to make beautiful things. The realization that we are called to be creative should inspire us not only to go to church, but also to visit museums. Better still, it should inspire us to take up the paint brush, enjoy literature, make music, take a course in photography, or try our hand at poetry. God the Creator is pleased if we exploit the creative talents He has given us.

### Stewards

One of the other clear messages of the Creation story is that humanity was appointed as God's housekeeper. We were given the privilege of being the stewards of God's creation. When modern Adventists hear the word *stewardship*, their first thought is of their checkbooks; sermons on stewardship will usually culminate in appeals to give a faithful tithe and more generous offerings. (Think about it for a moment. Why should we even need to be reminded to give our tithes? God's people in Old Testament times gave the tithe of their "increase." (How strange would it be if we were to give less than they did, considering the much grander revelation we have received from God and the fact that we know so much more about His plan of salvation?)

Being stewards of this earth has grave implications. How can it be that organizations such as Green Peace have left Seventh-day Adventists and most other evangelical Christians far behind when it comes to the care of our planet? We may not agree with many of the activities or ideas of the "greens" and other activists, but before we condemn them too strongly, we would do well to ask ourselves whether we have not often shamefully ignored our calling as stewards over the earth.

Bearing God's image certainly implies being a steward of His creation. It demands that we not only place a high value on human life, but also on other forms of life—in particular, those species of plants and animals that are threatened with extinction. It demands a lifestyle that shows a responsible use of natural resources, a conscious effort to reduce waste, and an eagerness to participate in recycling programs.

Moreover, being stewards of God's creation includes care of our own bodies and a healthy, balanced lifestyle. In general, Seventh-day Adventists perform better in this area than they do in most aspects of ecology. But quite a few of us still have a long way to go. Often we put into practice just a few aspects of healthy living, while largely ignoring other fundamental aspects. Tragically, it is not rare to find among Adventists ultra-strict vegetarians who ruin their health by being hopeless workaholics! Whatever they may think, they are not good stewards and, as a result, the image of God that is imprinted on them may lose at least some of its shine.

### Holy persons

In a world of sin nobody can be complacent about possessing the image of God. We cannot escape the unfortunate fact that large numbers of people have lost major chunks of their humanity. If anything of God's image is left in them, it is hidden under deep layers of egotism, materialism, or immorality—or a combination of these and other negative factors. In contrast with this group are those who continue to appreciate their status as creatures of the Almighty Creator and who want to respond to their Maker and are grateful for the divine image. Their highest ambition in life is to manifest and reflect this image of God more fully.

These people belong to God's "tribe." Though God expects them to continue to live in this world as ordinary, levelheaded citizens, they are separate from the rest of humanity in their ultimate goals and objectives. The biblical word for this separation is "holiness." These men and women, who appreciate the divine image and who want, more than anything else, to see this image reflected ever more clearly in what they say and do, are referred to as "holy" people.

Holiness is not synonymous with sinlessness. Unfortunately, total perfection can never be achieved in our present human condition. Holiness, as used in the Bible, describes a purpose rather than a state of being. Those who realize that they have been created in God's image will be steadfast in their determination to more consistently reflect His character and to be truly separate and among His holy people.

**Holy time**

These "holy" people, who want to be separate (in the positive sense referred to above!), have been entrusted with a very special gift that greatly assists them in better reflecting the divine image. When God made man, He also created time. He did so in sections of six-plus-one days. Right from the beginning there was separate time—holy time—to foster the unique bond between God and man.

The modern world would be a less materialistic and less stressful place to live, if more people today would remember this divinely instituted cycle of time and make sure to reserve holy time on the Sabbath day. People who not only want to retain God's image, but more than anything else want to see it shine forth in greater splendor, need holy time in their lives—time that is set aside to commune with God, both alone and with others who also want to worship Him on the day He has blessed. We also need this weekly holy day in order to have quality time with those we love and to recharge our spiritual batteries.

Making this weekly holy time part of the rhythm of life will prove to be a tremendous experience for anyone who tries it! God's special, weekly blessing is available to all!

### Fulfilling our potential

God is love. Therefore, if there is any aspect of God that is included in His image, it must be humanity's capacity for receiving and giving love—love for God, love for one another, love for a partner. Thank God for eros-love that enriches our human existence. And thank God also for His agape-love, which we, who bear His image, can reflect to those around us.

What then is this image of God all about? It is about fulfilling our God-given potential. To quote Macquarrie once more:

> We must think of the *imago Dei* more in terms of a potentiality for being that is given to man with his very being, than in terms of a fixed "endowment" or "nature". . . . [man] has an openness into which he can move outward and upward.[3]

*Moving outward and upward!* As we allow God to work in us, we can move outward and become a "significant other" (as psychologists would say) to more and more fellow human beings, and we can—gradually and often almost imperceptibly—grow in spiritual stature.

Knowing God as the one and only triune God, whose power, knowledge, and love know no limits, helps us to realize better what kind of God we are called to represent and are supposed to reflect—having been created in His image.

### Getting personal

Remember that we discussed in chapters six and seven that God is a person? That God has a name? That He wants a relationship with us? Not until I checked a concordance was I aware of how often God introduces

Himself as "the Lord, *your* God." Jeremiah 30:22 expresses what is found in the Bible dozens of times in similar words: " 'So you will be my people, and I will be your God.' " The Father of Jesus Christ is our Father, and His God is our God (see John 20:17). Therefore Jesus taught us to pray to God as "our Father" (Matthew 6:9).

God is not the far-away God who has retired since He set everything in motion with one big bang. He is involved in every aspect of our lives. What metaphor expresses this more poignantly than Jesus' assurance that God knows even how many hairs we have on our heads (see Matthew 10:30)? (In my case, that assurance is not so meaningful; perhaps I should take comfort from the fact that He knows exactly how many hairs I have lost!)

A strong personal tie is a solid basis for trust. We would entrust some people, whom we know well, with our life. If we can entrust ourselves, however, to anyone without any reservation, it is to this personal God of love. Trusting Him means that we do not entertain the slightest doubt that He is in control or that things never get out of [His] hand. Remember, what we earlier said of the larger picture that only an infinite God can survey?

This trust has both a micro- and a macro-dimension. God controls the details of every day of my life and your life. But He also controls the broad course of history. This is the basis for our trust in Bible prophecy. Our confidence does not primarily rest on historical research showing that past prophecies have come true; it rests, first of all, on what we know of the character of our God.

Having a personal God implies a wonderful intimacy between God and us. We can talk to Him as we would to a friend. Any Adventist knows the famous phrase: "Prayer is the opening of the heart to God as to a friend."[4]

The Jewish thinker Martin Buber (1878-1965) has exerted a strong influence on many Protestant theologians. Buber saw the essence of biblical Judaism in the ongoing dialogue between God and man. As long as God remains an *It*, we have not truly met the God of the Bible; only as God is encountered in a personal way as a *Thou*, can we claim to know Him.

This has struck a chord with many. And indeed an I-It religion cannot be more than a system of doctrines, whereas an I-Thou religion finds its fulfilment in an intimate relationship.

Prayer is the unique avenue for developing depth in this I-Thou relationship. In recent years, Adventists and other Christian writers have produced many good books on all imaginable aspects of prayer. So we will not devote much space to the subject in this book. Not because the topic is unimportant, but because there is so much excellent material so readily available.

Let me, however, say this: there are different kinds of prayer for different occasions, for different moods, for different times of the day or of the week, and even as we go through different phases of our lives. There is private prayer and the prayer of communal worship. All are important. The unfortunate truth is that many of us are not very good at prayer and should make a conscious effort to communicate better with God, just as many of us need better communication skills in our dealings with other people.

We may have intellectual questions about prayer. How can it possibly work? How can our petitions influence God to change His mind or how can we hope to twist His arm, if God is unchangeable? How do other people profit when we intercede for them in prayer? How fair is it that some people have the alleged advantage of having others pray for them, while others who are not mentioned in anyone's prayers, apparently miss out on the benefits of intercessory prayer? And must it not be utterly confusing for God when, as so often happens, at one and the same time the farmer prays for rain, while the person on vacation prays for sunshine? Whose prayer should God answer? I could add a great number of other awkward questions on this topic. But when everything is said and done, there is abundant proof that, in some miraculous way, prayer actually works. God wants us to pray. Somehow it fits into God's larger picture of things. And it does help us immensely in our spiritual growth.

In his insightful book *The Search for God—Can Science Help?*, Sir John Houghton, a prominent British scientist and a firm believer in God, sums up, better than I could, what I would want to say:

> For Christians, prayer is an expression of their relationship with God. It is the means whereby they, as God's children, communicate with God as their Father; how He speaks to them and they to Him. Because of this close relationship prayer is never far away. It is an attitude of mind through which they continually attempt to discover the will of God and to act upon it.[5]

**Responding to God's love**

Sir Houghton thereby points us to the next essential step in our faith journey. If we have truly understood our status as creatures who owe a response of trusting love (or loving trust) to our Creator, we will want to express this love in concrete action. Those who love God will be loyal to Him and to everything He asks. Nothing would be more natural for those who want to respond in love to their Creator than the desire to belong to the people "who obey God's commandments and remain faithful to Jesus" (Revelation 14:12). Seventh-day Adventists see it as their God-given task to point other believers to the challenge recorded in 1 John 2:3-5:

> We know that we have come to know him if we obey his commands [all of them]. The man who says, "I know him," but does not do what he commands is a liar, and the truth is not in him. But if anyone obeys his word, God's love is truly made complete in him. This is how we know we are in him.

Our love for God also finds expression in our love for other people—love for our neighbors, far and near. Love in the form of concrete help to those in need. Love, even when it is not returned. Love, also, for the unlovable. Love through ADRA, the Red Cross, UNICEF, and a thousand other charities. Love as a kind word to the bus driver or to the person next to us in a waiting room. Love as being there for others.

Our love is also expressed in our commitment to the community of believers to which we belong. Although faith is a very private thing, it grows by sharing. People with the same hope and the same outlook on life; people who have the same basic trust in the Christian Father-Son-and-Holy Spirit God, belong together and celebrate their faith and commitment together. A community of believers must be a center of love. If that is not the case, there is something terribly wrong.

Love for God is expressed in our private communion with God, but also in corporate worship. Those who have encountered the Almighty will want to praise Him, sing to His glory, listen together to His Word, and will want to share the bread and the wine as a regular reminder that the great I AM became God-with-us and through Christ saved us from our sins.

### Mission

Finally, love for God is expressed in mission. As we saw in the previous chapter, our experiential knowledge of the one and only true God must be shared. A true encounter with the Lord of the universe cannot leave us unconcerned about the fate of our fellow men.

The Seventh-day Adventist Church used to be a missionary-minded church. It no longer is—at least not to the extent it once was. We still give some of our money for the mission outreach of the church, but it is an ever smaller portion of our income and far less than we used to give. We spend fewer hours in missionary activities than a previous generation of Adventists did. Fewer of us are prepared to do front-line work in "unentered areas" or to accept assignments as long-term missionaries. Of course, these are generalizations. Many still make tremendous sacrifices, both in terms of time and financial resources. But overall trends are worrisome.

Some may want to approach this problem by suggesting that we should use state-of-the-art promotional techniques to challenge people to give more money. As they give, their interest in the church will grow, and as their interest in the church grows, their spiritual life will be enriched. No doubt, there is some truth in this. But the reverse order is far more natural. We need to focus on our own walk with God; then do what we can to point others to the joy of an intimate bond with our Creator. Once our spiritual life is put in order, missionary zeal will be the natural consequence, and we will want to give generously. Not all can go to Africa or Papua New Guinea, nor should we all go to such places. Not all of us have the talent to give Bible studies in a structured way. But we all have some resources and some talents that can be used in some aspect of ministry!

If we truly believe that God is our Maker; if we truly believe that He has solved our human predicament by giving Himself in His Son Jesus Christ; if we truly believe that our love to God finds its natural expression in obedience to the divine instructions given in God's Word; and if we truly believe that God will soon revisit this world in a climactic manner at the Second Coming of His Son—how, for God's sake, can we so often remain inactive and silent?

---

[1] John Macquarrie, *Principles of Christian Theology* (London: SCM Press, 1966), 212.
[2] Ellen G. White, "Wise and Unwise Marriages", *The Youth's Instructor*, 9 October, 1899.
[3] Macquarrie, 213.
[4] Ellen G. White, *Steps to Christ*, 93.
[5] John Houghton, *The Search for God—Can Science Help?* (Oxford: Lion Publishing plc, 1995), 162.

Epilogue

# In God We Trust

*How great is the love the Father has lavished on us, that we should be called children of God! And that is what we are!* (1 John 3:1).

There is no doubt: If God is our Father, then we are His children. We are sons and daughters of God, adopted into His family. Many Adventists seem to have difficulty in giving an immediate and straightforward answer to the question: "Are you a child of God?" Often the hesitant reply is: "I hope so." Or: "I think so." Or: "I try to be one."

Such answers are not good enough. What do we answer when somebody wants to know whether we are married? People would raise their eyebrows if we said: "I hope so." Or: "I think so." We know our marital status. We know what gender we are. We know what age group we belong to. We know what passport we hold. And we have every reason to be just as sure about our status in the family of God. God's Word ought to be good enough for us. " 'I will be a Father to you, and you will be my sons and daughters, says the Lord Almighty' " (2 Corinthians 6:18).

As God's children, we have the absolute assurance of salvation. May I quote one of my most favorite Bible passages? It says it all!

# OUR AWESOME GOD

> What, then, shall we say in response to this? If God is for us, who can be against us?. . . .
>
> Who shall separate us from the love of Christ? Shall trouble or hardship or persecution or famine or nakedness or danger or sword?
>
> As it is written: "For your sake we face death all day long; we are considered as sheep to be slaughtered."
>
> No, in all these things we are more than conquerors through Him who loved us.
>
> For I am convinced that neither death nor life, neither angels nor demons, neither the present nor the future, nor any powers, neither height nor depth, nor anything else in all creation, will be able to separate us from the love of God that is in Christ Jesus our Lord (Romans 8:31, 35-39).

Whatever happens, God is there for us. Nothing can separate us from His love. That is our assurance while in this present existence, but it also extends into the future beyond this life.

Most of us will be forgotten within a few decades after our death. At most, the memory of our existence will linger on in some gradually fading pictures in the family album. Fortunately, our future beyond death does not depend on any human memory, but on the glorious fact that the Almighty God, who knows everything and loves us with "everlasting love" (Jeremiah 31:3), remembers who we are.

Our return to life in the resurrection does not depend on some magic reconfiguration of the atoms and molecules of our present bodies. Scientists tell us that the physical makeup of our bodies changes constantly. We do not consist of the same matter we consisted of a decade or so ago. And after our death we truly return to dust. But, somehow, we are safe in God's memory. He remembers all the relevant data to recreate us when His time has come.

Yes, the character of God guarantees that we are safe even in death. We do not need to fear any judgment. If we make the right choice, to align ourselves with His kingdom, He will not let us down. He will pull us through. He will be there for us when it counts.

Reading this book, some may have felt that I seem not to attach too much significance to our traditional Adventist doctrines since I have not discussed them at any length. Such a conclusion would be incorrect. But I firmly believe that being a Seventh-day Adventist Christian does not begin with having all the right doctrines. It starts with knowing God. Believing and promoting the right doctrines, without having and sharing an experiential knowledge of the one and only true God, is idolatry.

Tony Ben (1925- ), a British Labour politician, said in a BBC interview in April 1989: "A faith is something you die for; a doctrine is something you kill for. There is all the difference in the world."

Indeed, doctrines without the Father-Son-Holy Spirit God of the Christian faith, who is our Creator and Redeemer, remain a dead letter. They result in opinions, possibly convictions and zeal, but not in true happiness and peace and a full assurance of salvation. When we have, however, established an intimate relationship with our God and, in spite of all our human limitations, gradually come to know Him better and better, our search for doctrinal truth will follow. We will want to know the implications of our faith in God, and we will want to do what He instructs us to do for our own good.

Like Job, we may have many questions. Like him, we may at times wonder where and what God is. But like him, we must come to the point in our spiritual journey that we can confidently say, " 'My ears had heard of you, but now my eyes have seen you' " (Job 42:5). Truly He is our awesome God!